INVITATIONAL TEACHING, LEARNING, AND LIVING

INVITATIONAL TEACHING, LEARNING, AND LIVING

William Watson Purkey
Paula Helen Stanley

nea PROFESSIONAL LIBRARY
National Education Association
Washington, D.C.

24247452
occ

12-13-91

Printing History
    First Printing: September 1991

Note

The opinions expressed in this publication should not be construed as representing the policy or position of the National Education Association. Materials published by the NEA Professional Library are intended to be discussion documents for educators who are concerned with specialized interests of the profession.

Library of Congress Cataloging-in-Publication Data

Purkey, William Watson.
    Invitational teaching, learning, and living / William Watson
Purkey, Paula Helen Stanley.
        p.   cm.—(Analysis and action series) 446
    Includes bibliographical references (p.   ).
    ISBN 0-8106-3049-4
    1. Teaching—Handbooks, manuals, etc.   2. Teaching—Aids and
devices—Handbooks, manuals, etc.   I. Stanley, Paula Helen.
II. Title. III. Series.
    LB1025.3.P87   1991
    371.1'02—dc20   91-26296
                                                                CIP

CONTENTS

Educating the mind without educating the heart is no education at all.

—*Aristotle*

The Authors

William Watson Purkey is Professor of Counselor Education at the University of North Carolina at Greensboro and Co-Founder and Co-Director of the International Alliance for Invitational Education. An active writer, lecturer, and researcher, Dr. Purkey is a frequent contributor to professional journals and is the author or co-author of many books on school achievement and success.

Paula Helen Stanley is Assistant Professor of Counselor Education at Radford University, Virginia.

The Advisory Panel

Sheri Bauman, Counselor, Centennial High School, Ft. Collins, Colorado

Carlita Beridon, Language Arts Teacher, Northwestern Middle School, Zachary, Louisiana

Neil Chivington, School Social Worker, School District #6, Buxton, Maine

H. Margaret Eaves, Reading Specialist, La Grange Independent School District, Texas

Kathy Fagan, Teacher, Baltimore County Public Schools, Maryland

Sandra Jacobson, Science Teacher, Ballou Junior High School, Puyallup, Washington

Robert Edward Johnson, Professor of Education, University of North Alabama, Florence

Joseph Sperlazza, Supervisor, Guidance and Alternative Programs, Jersey City Public Schools, New Jersey

Richard G. Stahlhut, Associate Professor of Teaching, University of Northern Iowa, Cedar Falls

PREFACE

Eeyore, the old grey Donkey, stood by the side of the stream, and looked at himself in the water.

"Pathetic," he said. "That's what it is. Pathetic."

He turned and walked slowly down the stream for twenty yards, splashed across it, and walked slowly back on the other side. Then he looked at himself in the water again.

"As I thought," he said. 'No better from this side. But nobody minds. Nobody cares. Pathetic, that's what it is."

—A. A. Milne
Winnie the Pooh *(76, p. 72)*

In light of the present outpouring of new "reform" programs, policies, mandates, commission reports, edicts, and legislation that focus almost entirely on school outcomes (as measured by multiple-choice tests), it seems pathetic ("That's what it is. Pathetic.") that so little attention is being given to a much more human concern: the emotional, affective, mentally and morally healthy side of the teaching/learning process.

A reform period is the best time for a revolution, and this book proposes a revolution: to make classrooms "the most inviting place in town," a place where teachers want to teach and students want to learn. When these wants are present, everything else will follow.

North America has unfathomed resources for great teachers and great students. These resources can be tapped in a totally facilitative and humane classroom culture. *Invitational Teaching, Learning, and Living* offers a model for the desired future based on the teacher's beliefs and behavior, working together. It provides a "world view" and a blueprint of what each teacher can do to improve the quality of teaching, learning, and living in every classroom.

As we present the framework of *Invitational Teaching, Learning, and Living*, we also offer practical strategies—each labeled IDEA:

Inviting
Descriptors of
Exciting
Activities

Each IDEA is designed to serve as a sampler of the countless ways teachers can apply *Invitational Teaching, Learning, and Living* in their personal and professional lives. Each IDEA can be used by any teacher, from kindergarten teachers through university professors, in any classroom. Here is a sample IDEA:

IDEA

USE ZEN KOANS: Zen masters use a special kind of question to invite their students to reflect deeply on one's self and one's relationship with the world. A koan is a simple question that has no simple answer. For example: "What is the sound of one hand clapping?" "What is love?" It is the student's struggle with the koan, rather than the teaching of the master, that enlightens the student.

A few of these IDEAs and background materials have been published previously in recent books and monographs dealing with invitational education, including *Inviting School Success* (93),* *The Inviting Relationship* (95), *Education: By Invitation Only* (94), and *Positive Discipline* (97). *Invitational Teaching, Learning, and Living* is different from these earlier books in that it focuses directly on the classroom teacher.

We invite you to validate this book against your own teaching experience and relationships with students of all ages. We welcome your comments and suggestions.

William Watson Purkey
Department of Counseling and
Specialized Educational Development
School of Education
University of North Carolina at Greensboro

Paula Helen Stanley
Radford University
Radford, Virginia

---

*Numbers in parentheses appearing in the text refer to the Bibliography beginning on page 87.

Chapter 1

WHAT IS INVITATIONAL TEACHING?

That is a beautiful occupation. And since it is beautiful, it is truly useful.

—*Antoine de Saint-Exupéry*
The Little Prince *(107, p. 59)*

According to a 1990 survey conducted by the Carnegie Foundation for the Advancement of Teaching (19), if given a second chance, many if not most, teachers would choose a different career. Counselors report "compassion fatigue," principals express "disillusionment," and students are seen as apathetic, passive, and uninterested. It is clear that there is a growing hunger in North American education for a more caring, exciting, engaging, and optimistic *zeitgeist* [zeit (time) and geist (spirit)]. Invitational teaching seeks to satisfy this hunger by making education a more satisfying and enriching experience for everyone involved in the teaching/learning process.

Invitational teaching is one aspect of an emerging model of education. The model, called "invitational education" (92, 93, 94, 95, 96, 97), is incomplete, with gaps unfilled and potentials unexplored.

Although invitational education is in its infancy, it is already providing a fresh conception of education—forming a new image of what teachers can do and what schools can become. Without a guiding image, education cannot be significantly improved. (See Figure 1.)

Figure 1

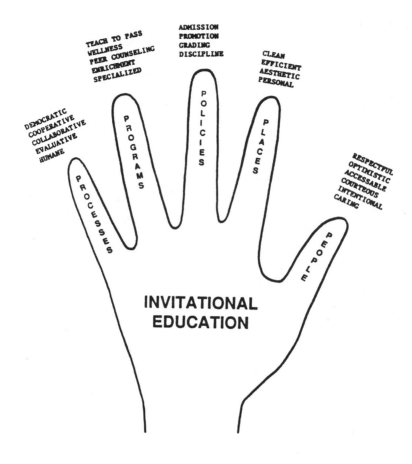

Invitational education proposes that people are able, valuable, and responsible and should be treated accordingly. It maintains that education is a cooperative activity in which process is as important as product. It proposes that individuals possess relatively untapped potential in all areas of human development. This potential can be realized through places, policies, and programs that are specifically designed to facilitate human development, and through people who are intentionally inviting with themselves and others, personally and professionally.

IDEA

KEEP IN TOUCH: It is essential that at least one adult in the school care about each student and take a special interest in that student. The care is demonstrated by keeping in frequent touch with the student and being available to others for consultation regarding the student's progress.

Invitational education is unlike any other model reported in the professional literature in that it addresses the global nature of schools, the entire school *gestalt* (an integrated whole, greater than the sum of its parts). It goes beyond other systems to consider the five vital *P*s: *places, policies, programs, processes,* and *people.* Its goal is to create a total school environment that intentionally summons people in schools to realize their relatively boundless potential in all areas of worthwhile human endeavor.

William Stafford of Lehigh University captured the essence of invitational education in a 1989 conversation with the authors: "Invitational Education has a much wider focus of application than is typically discussed in other self-theories. It is deliberately aimed at broader goals than students and their achievement alone. It is geared to the total development of all who interact within the school. It is concerned with more than grades, attendance, and even perceptions of self. It is concerned with the skills of becoming."

Invitational teaching is that part of invitational education that specifically addresses the vital role of the teacher in the teaching/learning process. It picks up where countless other programs and models leave off by providing an overarching guide for teaching. This guide makes explicit what has heretofore been implicit: that the primary goal of teaching is to cordially summon individuals to see themselves as able, valuable, and responsible and to behave accordingly. Invitational teaching provides a guiding framework for a variety of educational processes, programs, policies, places, and human activities that fit with the four basic elements of invitational education.

FOUR BASIC ELEMENTS

The four basic elements of invitational teaching are *trust, respect, optimism,* and *intentionality.* These elements give the teacher a consistent "stance" that can be used to create and maintain inviting actions, programs, policies, processes, and places. This stance provides a reliable internal compass that points to the true north of teaching: a therapeutic way of relating with oneself and others, personally and professionally.

Trust

Teaching is a cooperative, collaborative activity in which process is as important as product. Therefore, a basic ingredient of invitational teaching is a recognition of the interdependence of human beings. Attempting to get students to learn subject matter without involving them in the process is a lost cause. Even if the effort to teach students without their collaboration is successful, the energy expended is disproportionate to what is accomplished. Each student is ultimately responsible for his or her learning. Each student can learn, each student wants to learn, and when given an optimally inviting environment, each student will learn. Given an optimally inviting world, each student will find his or her own best ways of being and becoming.

> IDEA
>
> *MAKE COMMITMENTS:* Be willing to give your word, your say-so, that certain things will take place in the class. Giving your word that something will happen *in advance of guaranteed proof* gives you the momentum to do what it takes to make the commitment come true.

A study concerning teacher effectiveness by Bergman and Gaitskill (14) found that students ranked teachers' relationships with students first, above professional competence and personal attributes. Teachers who show they trust students also help underachievers perform better in school. Galbo (40) found that teachers who had the most significant influence on students developed personal relationships with them, communicated at the students' level, were understanding, showed interest, and interacted frequently. He found trust to be the critical factor in student/teacher interaction.

Research in fields other than education has shown that trust is a factor that influences the quality of effort given to a task. Ouchi (81) developed a model of successful management (theory Z) that emphasizes the obsolescence of adversarial management/employee relations and affirms the values of consensual decision making. Theory Z stresses mutual trust (implying minimal managerial supervision of employees) and collegiality based on respect. Theory Z is the forerunner of the presently popular "site-based management" and "faculty empowerment."

When invitational teaching is present, indications of trust are everywhere. Students are allowed to use equipment and assist with responsibilities, supervision is low-key, and rules are few and simple. Directions inform students what they are expected to do, not what they are forbidden to do.

Some teachers are so concerned about the prevention of vandalism or thievery that classrooms become prisons, with locks on everything and warning signs everywhere. The result is that vandals and thieves appear to be running the classroom, creating distrust in everyone. When chances of success are good, teachers who practice invitational teaching give students many opportunities to demonstrate their trustworthiness.

Respect

As Rogers explained so beautifully in his book *Freedom to Learn* (102), students can be trusted to learn and enjoy learning when the teacher creates and maintains a classroom environment that communicates respect through participation in selecting and reaching goals. People are able, valuable, and responsible and should be treated accordingly.

An indispensable ingredient in invitational teaching is shared responsibility based on mutual respect. This respect is manifested by the teacher's caring and appropriate behaviors, as well as by places, policies, programs, and processes created and maintained by teachers. Respect for people and respect for property are the foundations of invitational teaching.

According to Lewis (65), the most successful companies in the United States, including IBM, Hewlett-Packard, Delta Air Lines, and General Electric, have accomplished their successes by showing respect for their employees and customers. This respect is largely the result of a philosophy inculcated within the organization.

Hewlett-Packard's philosophy is called the HP Way and includes the following:

- Belief in people, freedom
- Respect and dignity, individual self-esteem
- Recognition, sense of achievement, participation
- Security, performance, development of people
- Sharing of benefits and responsibility, mutual help
- Decentralization
- Informality, open communications
- A chance to learn by making mistakes
- Training and education, counseling
- Performance and enthusiasm (65, p. 35)

Each of these principles indicates unconditional respect for employees and their capabilities and talents, and each can be applied to the classroom setting.

The importance of respect is also underscored by educational research. In a series of research studies (5, 48, 61, 99, 109, 111) involving more than 2,000 secondary and postsecondary students, a consistently high correlation was reported among indicators of invitational teaching (such as trust, respect, optimism, and intentionality) and student affective outcomes (such as attitudes toward the course, subject matter, teacher, and self-as-learner). Creating a classroom environment based on mutual respect appears to be a highly effective way of encouraging student achievement. Arnold and Roach (6) in their study of nonverbal behaviors of teachers, found that teachers who

19

exhibited respect for students by starting and ending class on time tended to have students who viewed the class as important and therefore studied more.

IDEA

BE A CLOCK WATCHER: Promptness on the teacher's part establishes a sense of "on time" performance and shows respect for students and academic subject matter. A small clock within easy view in the classroom or office will help the teacher to start and end sessions on time. It also avoids the problem of going over the time period and inconveniencing students and other teachers.

Nonverbal teacher behaviors that indicate lack of respect for students (as perceived by students) include being late for class; making little or no eye contact; speaking without expression when lecturing; looking at one's watch; and staring at books, notes, the floor, or the chalkboard (6). These behaviors give students the message that the teacher does not know the subject matter, does not like teaching, and does not care if students learn anything. It is important in invitational teaching to communicate that students and learning are respected.

Goffin (41) suggested that teachers show respect for students by developing an appreciation for each student's uniqueness and intelligence. She stressed the importance of using discipline not as punishment, but as an opportunity to explore alternative behaviors that show respect for others. Bergman and Gaitskill (14), in a study of characteristics of effective teachers, found that effective teachers showed respect for students, maintained realistic expectations, offered helpful feedback, and encouraged students to ask questions. The same approach was advocated by Purkey and Strahan (97) in their work with "disconnected" students.

20

An example of encouraging respect in the classroom was given by Clyde Lovelady, a former graduate student at the University of North Carolina at Greensboro and an experienced classroom teacher:

> Jerry wouldn't take care of my plants most of the year. I asked him to water them, and he told me to do it myself. I begged him to feed my plants, and he laughed at me and shook his shaggy red head. One hot spring day, I started to hang three plants next to the window so they could get plenty of sun. Jerry commented on the transfer of these precious plants. "Mr. Lovelady, why are you hanging those ferns next to the window?" Looking at Jerry, I answered in my well-cultivated teacher logic. "Why Jerry, the sun supplies the essence of life. All living creatures, be they human, monkey, plants, or some form of primordial ooze and slime, need light and warmth." Jerry rolled his eyes and countered—"But Mr. Lovelady, ferns thrive better in shade than sunlight. If you leave those ferns there, they will turn yellow. Let me take care of your plants. You don't know how." Henceforth, Jerry was commissioned "Lord Jerry, Protector of His Majesty's Plants." My plants did well those last few weeks of school . . . and so did Jerry.

Landfried (62) described behaviors of teachers that demonstrated lack of respect and encouraged students to behave irresponsibly. These behaviors included not holding students accountable for academic performance, giving assignments that were "too easy," allowing students to show disrespect for the teacher and others in the classroom, and doing things for students they could do for themselves. Landfried proposed that these teacher behaviors teach students that they can neglect deadlines, demand good grades with little effort, expect others to solve their problems, believe mediocrity is a worthwhile goal, and create low goals for themselves. Practicing invitational teaching does not mean that the teacher gives up high expectations for every student. Respect in action is exhibited by one high school teacher who has a full-length mirror in the classroom with the caption "Please act as good as you look."

A corollary of respecting others is asking for respect in turn. The teacher has the perfect right to expect respect from students. When the teacher neglects to assert his or her own value and ability, it is difficult for students not to take advantage of the situation. A major component of invitational teaching is respect for self as well as respect for others.

Optimism

People possess untapped potential in all areas of human endeavor. Invitational teaching could not be seriously considered if optimism did not exist. No one in a school—not a teacher, student, principal, counselor, supervisor, or whoever—can choose a beneficial direction in life without hope that change for the better is possible.

There are a few teachers who find value in pessimism and cynicism. But Erica Jong in her book, *How to Save Your Own Life*, places cynicism in a different light: "Many people today believe that cynicism requires courage. Actually, cynicism is the height of cowardice. It is innocence and open-heartedness that require the true courage—however often we are hurt as a result of it" (53, p. 97).

Optimism is critical in invitational teaching because teachers create the facts that make their hypotheses come true. If the teacher believes that some students don't want to learn, they won't. If the teacher believes students have the ability to learn, they will. The axiom of invitational teaching is that students live up, or down, to the teacher's expectations. Sometimes the student the teacher would least expect to be receptive can, when given the right invitation, be the most receptive one in the classroom.

Research indicates that the more students believe they will succeed if they practice (16), and the more they sense positive regard from significant others (45), the higher their self-esteem is and the more they are likely to practice.

Good and Brophy (42) reported that teachers tend to treat low and high achievers differently based on their expectations of these students' likelihood of success. Teachers give low achievers less time to answer a question and more often criticize low achievers for failure. Teachers tend to give low achievers less eye contact, are less friendly, smile less, and give them fewer nonverbal signals of support. These teacher behaviors are important because they indicate the teacher's level of optimism for student achievement.

As an example of the influence of optimism, one high school student wrote: "Mr. Penn invited us to like ourselves and take pride in our work. He expected a great deal of us and we did not let him down. He thought we were brighter than we were, so we were." Optimism, as reflected in the behavior of such teachers as Mr. Penn, is based on a cardinal principle of invitational teaching: Human potential, though not always apparent, is always there, waiting to be discovered and invited forth.

An important corollary of optimism is that everything counts. No place, policy, program, process, or person is neutral. Everything a teacher does, as well as *how* he or she does it, adds or detracts from success. The classroom appearance, the discipline policy, the academic program, the organizational process, and the actions of people all contribute to success or failure in the classroom—all telegraph optimism or pessimism regarding students and their abilities.

Invitational teaching assumes that every student is the world's greatest authority on something and that every student is an expert on a number of things. It also assumes that every student can learn, and wants to learn, and that every student can be taught. When teachers look at nonreaders and see readers, look at nonscientists and see scientists, look at nonartists and see artists, then success is likely to be realized.

A beautiful example of optimism was given to one of the authors by a former student body president at the University of North Carolina at Greensboro. She reported that her interest in politics began unexpectedly in her junior year of high school:

> One day between class change I was chatting with a teacher about the upcoming class elections. We were talking about who would make a good class president. I named two or three of the usual class leaders (the ones that glitter when they walk). After I named the leaders, the teacher looked at me and said: "And what about you?" I rolled in the aisle! That was the craziest thing I'd ever heard. I had never been elected to anything in my whole life. Three weeks later, after I had been elected class president, the teacher and I laughed about the conversation we had between class change.

The uniqueness of human beings is that no clear limits to potential have been discovered. The optimistic view of seeing people as possessing untapped potential in all areas of human endeavor determines the curricula devised, the policies established, the programs supported, the processes encouraged, and the physical environments created and maintained.

Intentionality

By definition, an invitation is an intentional act designed to offer something beneficial for consideration. The more intentional the teacher is, the more accurate his or her judgments and the more decisive his or her behavior. As Peck noted in *The Road Less Traveled* (89), "the person who truly loves does so because of a decision to love" (p. 119). Intentionality leads to direction and control in one's personal and professional life.

An example of intentionality in action was given by a college student who wrote: "When I was in the fifth grade I was very sick and almost died. My teacher called our home every day. Later when I returned to school, he helped me catch up. I'll always remember his kindness, and someday I hope to write a book which says: 'Dedicated to Mr. Norman Siegal.'"

Short and Short (108) found a significant relationship between the teacher's deliberate actions and students' on-task behaviors. Students were more likely to get involved and show attention to learning activities when they perceived teachers as clearly communicating caring about students' successes in learning and clearly providing classroom structure and responsibility.

One additional reason for intentionality is that it helps teachers generate alternate choices and approaches to given situations. As Ivey (50) noted, intentional individuals are able to develop plans, act on many possible opportunities, and evaluate the effect of these actions. It takes intentionality to consistently and dependably offer something beneficial for consideration, particularly in the face of major difficulties and apparent rejection.

IDEA

BE WITH IT: Make a special effort to understand (but not emulate) the world of today's students. Try to keep abreast of fads, fashions, heroes, films, sports, actors, singers, music, and other current interests of students. Using an example from a student's "real life" is a powerful way to invite learning and encourage interest in academic content.

The value of intentionality is revealed in one student's successful change in behavior, as described by Purkey and Strahan (97).

Keith was one of those students "whose reputation preceded him" to the middle school. His elementary teachers passed along horror stories of his escapades: the day he inked his hands to leave a trail of blue prints along the white walls of his third grade classroom, the time in fourth grade when he used his scissors to "trim" the hair of a girl seated in front of him, his record number of trips to the principal's office in fifth grade. According to records, his previous teachers had tried everything from conferring, consulting, and confronting, to detention, demerits, and deterrents—all to no avail.

When the sixth grade teacher learned that Keith would be one of his students in the fall, he began to plan for success. Several weeks before the start of the new school year he sent a card to all of his incoming students (including a *special* note to Keith) welcoming them to his class. Next, he studied Keith's records and found not only an abundance of referrals but also a number of indications of academic potential.

On the first day of class, students were asked to complete autobiographical inventories describing their interests. Keith listed "pets" and "reading" among his likes. When Keith interrupted class discussion with, "Hey, did you hear about the guy who tried to dry his hat in the microwave?" the teacher waved off his comment and moved closer to him. A second disruption was greeted by the teacher with "We will talk about this after class."

During the private conference the teacher explained his expectations for the class and asked Keith to talk about his expectations as well. During the conference the teacher also asked Keith to help him set up a class aquarium. After the aquarium was operating, the teacher encouraged Keith to join several students as tutors in a reading program for younger students. Maintaining the aquarium and serving as a tutor helped Keith feel a part of the class and assisted him in improving his behavior. Keith acted up from time to time, but the teacher's intentional efforts were successful in improving the student's behavior. (pp 6–7)

In the situation with Keith, invitational teaching is visible. The teacher worked to develop a relationship based on mutual *trust* and *respect*. The teacher was *optimistic* that Keith could learn self-discipline and was *intentional* with a plan of action. At its best, invitational teaching can overcome years of unruly student behavior.

SUMMARY

This opening chapter has introduced invitational teaching, which is based on trust, respect, optimism, and intentionality. Teachers who adopt invitational teaching exhibit their *trust* by consistently providing opportunities for students to make decisions that count. These teachers manifest *respect* by encouraging students to see themselves as able, valuable, and responsible and to behave accordingly. They demonstrate *intentionality* by maintaining consistency in purpose and direction. And, finally, they maintain *optimism*, which brightens the darkest moments and makes teaching worthwhile. Chapter 2 offers a detailed look at the foundations of invitational teaching: the perceptual tradition and self-concept theory.

Chapter 2

FOUNDATIONS OF INVITATIONAL TEACHING

> *It is as if an army of mad botanists had gone out to collect plants . . . without any effort to find out what the family interrelationships were among the various collected items.*
>
> —*W. R. Uttal*
> A Taxonomy of Visual Processes
> *(112, p. 245)*

Data proliferation in education is everywhere. Never before in North American education has there been such an outpouring of research findings. State, provincial, regional, national, and international journals by the hundreds report the findings of countless thousands of researchers. What is now desperately needed is a cognitive framework for the incredible amount of empirical data piling up in professional libraries.

Fortunately, invitational teaching is based on two successive foundations that provide it with an overarching logical framework and a coherent structure that give order to myriad research findings. This chapter presents an overview of these two foundations: the perceptual tradition and self-concept theory. The pyramid in Figure 2 illustrates how these foundations support invitational teaching.

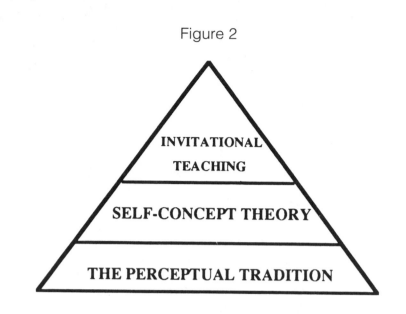

Figure 2

THE PERCEPTUAL TRADITION

> Our perceptions of ourselves and the world are so real to us that we seldom pause to doubt them. Since persons behave in terms of their personal perceptions, effective helping must start with the helper's understanding of the nature and dynamics of perceiving. (28, p. 15)

At the base of invitational teaching is the perceptual tradition. This tradition maintains that human behavior is the product of how individuals view the world. The perceptual tradition was beautifully presented in the classic *Perceiving, Behaving, Becoming* (23), edited by A. W. Combs for the Association for Supervision and Curriculum Development. In this book, individuals are viewed from "the internal frame of reference"—which means viewing humans as they themselves normally view the world.

The term *perceptual* refers not only to the senses, but also to meanings—the personal significance of events for the experiencing person. This perceptual process transcends sensations to include feelings, desires, purposes, explanations, and aspirations.

The perceptual tradition stands in contrast to other theoretical viewpoints that depict human behavior as basically a complex bundle of stimuli and responses or the product of a host of unconscious urges and suppressed desires. Rather than "objective" reality or "unconscious" forces, the perceptual tradition gives primary importance to each individual's perceived world.

The focus of this monograph does not permit recognition of the many researchers and scholars who have contributed to the perceptual tradition. However, special recognition should be given to George Herbert Mead (72), Gordon Allport (1, 2, 3, 4), Arthur W. Combs (22, 23, 24, 25, 27, 28, 29, 30), George Kelly (58, 59), C. H. Patterson (82, 84, 86, 87, 88), and Carl Rogers (100, 101, 103, 104), all of whom were major contributors to the perceptual tradition.

Some basic assumptions of the perceptual tradition have been identified by Purkey and Schmidt (95):

1. There may be a preexistent reality, but each individual can only know that part which comprises his or her perceptual world, the world of awareness.
2. All experiences are phenomenal in character: The fact that two individuals share the same physical environment does not mean that they have the same experiences.
3. Perceptions at any given moment exist at countless levels of awareness, from the vaguest to the sharpest.
4. Because people are limited in what they can perceive, they are highly selective in what they *choose* to perceive.
5. What individuals *choose* to perceive is determined by past experiences as mediated by present purposes, perceptions, expectations, and aspirations.
6. Individuals tend to perceive only that which is

relevant to their purposes and make their choices accordingly.

7. Choices are determined by perceptions, not facts. How a person acts is a function of his or her perceptual field at the moment of acting.

8. No perception can ever be fully shared or totally communicated because it is embedded in the life of the individual.

9. "Phenomenal absolutism" means that people tend to assume that others perceive as they do. If others perceive differently, it is often thought to be because others are mistaken or because they lie.

10. The perceptual field, including the perceived self, is internally organized and personally meaningful. When this organization and meaning are threatened, emotional problems are likely to result.

11. People not only perceive the world of the present, they also reflect on past experiences and imagine future ones to guide their behavior.

12. Beliefs can and do create their own social reality. People respond with feelings not only to "reality," but to their perceptions of reality.

13. Reality can exist for an individual only when he or she is conscious of it and has some relationship with it.

14. Communication depends on the process of acquiring greater mutual understanding of one another's phenomenal fields. (p. 30)

These fourteen assumptions are based on the premise that all behavior is a function of the individual's perceptual field. A student's (or teacher's) behavior may make little or no sense when observed from an external viewpoint, but the same behavior makes perfect sense when understood through the eyes of the perceiving, behaving individual.

An example of reading behavior backwards was provided by a very tall first grade teacher who had the habit of squatting down to talk to students at eye level. One day while on playground duty she approached a group of kindergartners and squatted to talk with them. They immediately squatted, too! The teacher's behavior was perceived by the kindergartners as an invitation to squat.

IDEA

READ BEHAVIOR BACKWARDS: Rather than looking only at behavior, consider how the behaving person might be viewing self, others, and the world. By looking at the *why* of behavior, it is much easier to understand the *what.*

Invitational teaching offers the classroom teacher the opportunity to "read behavior backwards," to realize that behavior is a function of the perceptions that exist for the student at the moment of behaving. By recognizing that human behavior is always a product of how people view their world, teachers can work to influence these perceptions. When students perceive the teacher as caring and supportive, view course content as important, and perceive themselves as valuable, responsible, and capable, then learning will occur.

Because of the contributions of perceptually oriented researchers, such as Aspy's perceptual characteristics of effective helpers (7), Meichenbaum's perceived self-efficacy studies (73, 74), Chamberlin's "preflections" of the future (20), Mahoney's "constructive ontology" (69), and Beck and Emery's "cognitive constellation" (12), the perceptual tradition continues to provide strong support for invitational teaching. The perceptual tradition also serves as a major foundation for self-concept theory.

SELF-CONCEPT THEORY

Linus: Look Sally, when I cut this apple in half, I have two halves.

Sally: That's fractions!!! I can't do fractions!! Fractions are too hard!

Linus: (sighs) I certainly don't envy teachers their lot.

—Charles Shulz, *Peanuts*

The second level of the pyramid is self-concept theory. After decades of neglect, self-concept is enjoying renewed attention from researchers. Scientists from many disciplines are discovering that self-concept gives consistency and predictability to the entire human personality.

One major figure who consistently kept sight of the importance of self-concept was Carl Rogers. In Rogers's view, the self-concept is *the* central ingredient in human personality and personal adjustment. Rogers described the self as a social product developing out of interpersonal relationships. He maintained that the self strives for consistency and proposed that there is a basic human need for positive regard both from others and from oneself. A major contribution of Rogers was his vision that in every human being there is a tendency toward self-actualization so long as it is allowed by the environment.

Other early contributors to self-concept theory include Cooley (31), Patterson (83, 85), Wylie (115, 116), Fitts, (39), Coopersmith (32), Piers and Harris (90), Jourard (54, 55), Kohut (60), and Harter (45). In addition, a number of recent studies (8, 18, 46, 75) have made significant advances in understanding the nature and importance of self-concept.

The vital role of self-concept as a possible causal agent in academic achievement was presented by Midkiff, Burke, Hunt, and Ellison (75) in their research on the role of self-concept of academic attainment in school achievement. They concluded that students' post-performance self-concepts of academic

34

attainment were influenced primarily by their initial self-concepts of academic attainment and, to lesser extent, by their academic achievement and performance on an academic task.

Helmke (46), in a study of children's self-concept of ability and mathematical achievement, found that students with high self-concepts had expectations of success, rather than a fear of failure. They persisted longer at a task, despite boredom, lack of interest in assigned work, and mistakes made. Students with low self-concepts were more likely during tests to have task-irrelevant cognitions that interfered with their ability to perform well. Clawson and Paterno (21) reported that the connection between self-concept as learner and school achievement forms as early as first grade.

Self-concept may be defined as the totality of a complex and dynamic system of learned beliefs that each individual holds to be true about his or her personal existence. This belief system provides consistency in personality and predictability in behavior. Self-concept has at least five characteristics: It is (1) organized, (2) dynamic, (3) consistent, (4) modifiable, and (5) learned.

IDEA

SHOW AND TELL: When done caringly and appropriately, "show and tell" works well with any group of students. You ask students: "Among your personal treasures, what is there that says something about you?" Invite students to bring their mementos to school and share them during a "sharing" session. By talking about their treasures, they are really talking about themselves. It is an effective way to get students to know each other on a more personal level.

Organized

Self-concept researchers (26, 32, 44, 45, 64, 70, 90, 116) agree that the self is characterized by internal harmony and orderliness. Anyone who has ever said, "Oh, I could *never* do that," can understand how each person strives to maintain an organization of internal beliefs and external behavior. Individual personality is far more than a hodgepodge of ideas; it is a road map for living. Without this internal organization and direction, human personality would be difficult to imagine.

Dynamic

A second quality of self-concept is that it is dynamic. Combs and his associates (23, 28, 30) maintained that the maintenance, protection, and enhancement of the perceived self (one's own personal existence as viewed by the perceiving individual) are the basic conditions behind all human behavior. For example, suppose a student sees him- or herself as incapable of learning algebra. Because of the dynamic nature of the self, the student creates the facts that make his or her perceptions come true. The student does not study because he or she believes one *cannot* learn algebra . . . and subsequently fails. Paradoxically, being right, even about being a poor student, has reward value: "See, I told you I was no good at algebra!"

Consistent

Individuals require a certain amount of internal consistency. Without this consistency, a stable personality would be difficult to imagine. From a lifetime of analyzing one's own behaviors and the reactions of others to that behavior, each person acquires expectations about what actions are appropriate. When an individual behaves in a manner that appears inconsistent with the self, a state of discomfort develops. This discomfort, according to Festinger (38), occurs when one behaves in a way that is not in keeping with one's self-concept. To avoid discomfort, students cling to their perceptions of themselves, no matter how detrimental these perceptions might be.

An example of self-concept consistency in action was provided by one of the author's junior high school students who thought of himself as a very poor student. He insisted on seeing himself as such in spite of ample evidence to the contrary. He would even sabotage his own good work to maintain his self-image as a poor student.

Modifiable

As noted earlier, the self-concept is more than a sum total of perceptions. It is an active and continuous flow of thoughts and feelings. In each reasonably healthy person, new ideas filter into the self-concept throughout the life span, while old ideas drift away. This constant flow allows for infinite modifiability of the perceived self and relatively boundless potential for the realization of human potential.

It is useful here to pause and consider the nature of human motivation from an invitational teaching viewpoint. According to Combs and Snygg (30), Avila and Purkey (10), Purkey, (91), Purkey and Novak (93), and others, there is only a single kind of motivation. This is an internal and continuous drive that every individual has at all times, in all places, during any activity. It is a "given." Rather than thinking of ways to *motivate* students, teachers who employ invitational teaching spend their time thinking of ways to *invite* students to be able, valuable, and responsible and to behave accordingly. "Motivate" implies a doing *to*. "Invite" implies a doing *with*. The difference is the heart of invitational teaching.

Understanding human motivation from an invitational teaching perspective gives teachers a profound advantage. By assuming that motivation is a basic force that is already present and that comes from within, teachers can use their energies in seeking "doing with" rather than "doing to" activities. A "doing with" relationship sets the stage for a cooperative spirit of mutual learning.

Learned

An overarching assumption of self-concept theory is that people become the ways they perceive themselves as being treated. If persons feel loved, it is because they perceive the love of others. If students feel neglected, it is because they perceive themselves as being neglected. If students feel able or unable in the classroom, it is because of perceived classroom experiences. Students develop confidence as learners when they perceive their efforts to be successful—whether it be answering a question correctly, or making a small step toward understanding some concept or idea, or working productively and cooperatively with others.

IDEA

CUT THE DECK: A good way to encourage class participation and cooperation is to divide and subdivide the class. Start out with pairs, then groups of four, and later groups of eight and sixteen. It is difficult for a student to remain silent on a subject when he or she is 50 percent of the group. This process sets the stage for active participation and invites everyone to contribute.

From an invitational teaching perspective, it is surprising that so many educational researchers have spent incredible amounts of time, energy, and money trying to improve education without recognizing that teacher and student perceptions of themselves, others, and the world are significantly related to school achievement. These perceptions are also related to a host of other educational concerns, such as the "at risk" student, the dropout, and the "discipline problem."

IDEA

USE YOUR SELF AS AN INSTRUMENT: The most important teaching instrument in any classroom is the classroom teacher. Use of the teacher's self is the process of combining knowledge, skills, and understanding into his or her own unique ways of functioning. The creative use of oneself is the best way to ensure an inviting classroom.

SUMMARY

This chapter has presented the two successive layers of the pyramid on which invitational teaching rests: the perceptual tradition and self-concept theory. Proponents of the perceptual tradition understand human behavior from an "internal" viewpoint—through the eyes of the experiencing, perceiving individual. Self-concept theory is that part of perception in which the focus is on the individual's awareness and interpretation of his or her personal existence. It is life observing itself. This self-concept gives consistency and predictability to the entire human personality.

Chapter 3 will consider four levels of invitational teaching: (1) intentionally disinviting, (2) unintentionally inviting, (3) unintentionally disinviting, and (4) intentionally inviting. Chapter 3 will also introduce the magical "plus factor" in teaching.

Chapter 3

FOUR LEVELS OF FUNCTIONING

"What makes the desert beautiful," said the Little Prince, "is that somewhere it hides a well . . ."

—*Antoine de Saint-Exupéry*
The Little Prince *(107, p. 93)*

In addition to centering on the four elements of trust, respect, optimism, and intentionality and basing itself on the perceptual tradition and self-concept theory, invitational teaching identifies levels of functioning that provide an informal check system for personal and professional teaching, learning, and living. Everyone functions at each level from time to time, but it is the level at which one typically functions that determines one's life style and success or failure in one's personal and professional teaching, learning, and living.

It is useful to pause here and contemplate the complexity of invitational teaching. Many teachers think they already understand the concept of "inviting." They see it as simply doing nice things—sharing a smile, giving a hug, saying something nice, or buying a gift. But invitational teaching is far more than giving "warm fuzzies," sharing "strokes," forming "hug stations," or walking around with IALAC sheets. While these are worthwhile activities when used caringly and appropriately, they are only manifestations of a theoretical "stance" one takes. This stance for invitational teaching (trust, respect, optimism, and intentionality as presented in Chapter 1) determines the level of personal and professional functioning.

There are many ways to categorize teacher behaviors. Invitational teaching identifies four categories: level 1, intentionally disinviting; level 2, unintentionally disinviting; level 3, unintentionally inviting; and level 4, intentionally inviting. When one reaches and consistently inhabits level 4, then the "plus factor" comes into play. It will be useful to look at these levels more closely.

INTENTIONALLY DISINVITING

The most negative and toxic level of human functioning involves those actions, policies, programs, places, and processes that are designed to demean, dissuade, discourage, defeat, and destroy. People who function at this bottom level deliberately send messages to themselves and others that they are unworthy, incapable, and irresponsible. Examples of intentionally disinviting functioning might be a teacher who is intentionally insulting, a policy that is deliberately discriminatory, a program that purposely demeans students, or an environment that is intentionally left unpleasant and unattractive.

After attending a workshop on invitational education, a teacher sent a note to the principal, pointing out that the girls' restroom needed soap, paper towels, and tissue. Her note was returned to her mailbox at the end of the day with this remark written across the bottom (unsigned): "What do you think this place is—the Hilton?" With such an intentionally disinviting stance, is it any wonder that students in this particular school are so apathetic or unruly or that the school has the reputation of being one of the worst in the state?

Intentionally disinviting teachers may behave as they do because of their own sense of inadequacy, low self-concept, or unfulfillment. Perhaps they are miserable and seek to make the lives of others miserable as well. They may have lost all hope in the value of human compassion or in their ability to affect others and situations positively. These teachers may need counseling or other assistance to deal with their hurtful existence. But whether because of racial prejudice, sadistic impulse, basic distrust, feelings of worthlessness, or unrequited love, there is no justification for teachers to function at the intentionally disinviting level.

UNINTENTIONALLY DISINVITING

People, places, policies, programs, and processes that are intentionally disinviting are rare when compared to those at the unintentionally disinviting level. Most unintentionally disinviting factors in and around classrooms are the result of a lack of stance. Because there is no philosophy of trust, respect, optimism, and intentionality, policies are established, programs designed, places arranged, and behaviors exhibited that are clearly disinviting, although such was not the intent.

The teachers who typically function at the unintentionally disinviting level spend a lot of time wondering: "Why do I have such a low attendance rate?" "Why are the students so unhappy in this classroom?" "Why are our achievement scores so low?" "Why don't I enjoy my teaching more?" The answers may lie in the teacher's unintentionally disinviting behaviors. The answers may also lie in unintentionally disinviting school policies over which the teacher has little control.

IDEA

REHEARSE THE FUTURE: Often when we make mistakes, we tend to go over them again and again: "How could I be so stupid?" It is better to ask: "How will I handle such things better in the future?" By thinking of positive future responses, reviewing past mistakes can be beneficial.

Teachers are sometimes caught in a bind by school policies that are unintentionally disinviting. Dworkin, Haney, Dworkin, and Telschow (36) note that teachers often lack the power to make important decisions concerning students. They have to wait for decisions to filter down from the administrative hierarchy. Parents and students then blame teachers for being indecisive. Moreover, teachers can experience conflict between what colleges of education teach them about teaching and what school boards, central administrations, and principals will permit them to do (36). Fortunately, with recent national attention being given to "site-based management" and "teacher empowerment," teachers are acquiring a larger voice in decisions that concern the teaching/learning process.

Examples of unintentionally disinviting forces can be seen in almost any school: the sign that reads NO STUDENTS ALLOWED IN SCHOOL BEFORE 8:15 A.M. (although the temperature is below zero), the policy of reserving the best parking space for the principal, the tendency to answer the office phone with a curt "Jackson Junior," and teachers who consistently kick students "in the but" ("This is a good paper, Mary, but . . ."). Teachers who function at the unintentionally disinviting level do not intend to be disinviting, but the damage is done. It is like being hit by a careless truck driver: Intended or not, the victim is still injured or killed. Those who function at the unintentionally disinviting level may be well meaning, but their behavior is often seen by others as chauvinistic, condescending, patronizing, or just plain thoughtless.

A sad example of unintentionally disinviting teacher behavior was shared by a student who chose "The Charge of the Light Brigade" to memorize for an English class assignment. After the student presented her poem with verve and enthusiasm, the teacher commented, "Good work, Barbara, but you should have selected a poem appropriate for a girl."

UNINTENTIONALLY INVITING

Teachers who typically function at the unintentionally inviting level have stumbled serendipitously into ways of functioning that are often effective. However, when asked to explain their philosophy of education, they have difficulty. They can describe in loving detail *what* they do, but not *why*. "Natural born" teachers are an example of this. They are successful in teaching because they exhibit many of the trusting, respecting, and optimistic qualities associated with invitational teaching. But because they lack the fourth critical element, *intentionality*, they lack consistency and dependability in the actions they exhibit, the policies and programs they establish, the processes they employ, and the places they create and maintain.

Young teachers often fall into the unintentionally inviting trap. While they are likable, entertaining, and enthusiastic, and they graduated just in time to save education, they lack intentionality regarding *why* they are doing what they do. The basic weakness in functioning at the unintentionally inviting level lies in the inability to identify the reasons for success or failure. Teachers can usually tell whether something is working or not, but when something stops working, some teachers are puzzled about how to start it up again. Those who function at the unintentionally inviting level lack a consistent stance—a dependable position from which to operate.

Teachers who are unintentionally inviting are somewhat akin to the early barnstorming airplane pilots. These pioneer pilots did not know much about the principles of aerodynamics and why their planes flew, what caused weather patterns, or why there was a need for navigational systems. As long as they stayed close to the ground, following a road or railway track, and as long as the weather was clear, they were able to function. But when night fell or the weather turned bad, they quickly landed or became disoriented and lost. In difficult situations, those who function at the unintentionally inviting level lack dependability in behavior and consistency in direction. Invitational teaching requires the creation and maintenance of a consistently inviting stance, even in the rain, which brings us to a fourth level of functioning: intentionally inviting.

INTENTIONALLY INVITING

When teachers function at the intentionally inviting level they seek to consistently exhibit the essential elements of invitational teaching presented in Chapter 1. A beautiful example of an intentionally inviting teacher is presented by Mizer (77), who described how schools can function to turn a child "into a zero." Mizer illustrated the tragedy of one such child and then concluded her article with these words:

I look up and down the rows carefully each September at the unfamiliar faces. I look for veiled eyes or bodies scrounged into an alien world. "Look, Kids," I say silently, "I may not do anything else for you this year, but not one of you is going to come out of here a nobody. I'll work or fight to the bitter end doing battle with society and the school board, but I won't have one of you coming out of here thinking of himself as a zero." (77, p. 10)

Intentionality can be a tremendous asset for teachers, for it serves as a constant reminder of the truly important parts of teaching.

O'Keefe and Johnson (80) noted that teachers who are intentionally inviting are more likely to be responsive to their students. These teachers read "students' cues and characteristics and 'flex' to individual students or groups by adjusting communication accordingly. . . . What seems to distinguish the highly adaptive teacher is the capacity to see beneath the external behavioral cues and to recognize the unique psychological qualities of each interaction" (80, p. 20). The research of Wigington, Tollefson, and Rodriguez (113) indicates a bonus aspect of intentionally inviting behavior: Teachers who received higher ratings from students were those who carefully and deliberately encouraged active learning and class participation.

In invitational teaching, *everybody* and *everything* adds to, or subtracts from, connecting with students. Ideally, the factors of people, places, policies, programs, and processes should be so intentionally inviting as to create a classroom where each individual is cordially summoned to develop physically, intellectually, and psychologically. Even a "Quote of the Day" by a famous person or a student, placed on the chalkboard, can signal the teacher's intentionally inviting stance. Those who accept the basic assumptions of invitational teaching not only strive to be intentionally inviting, but once there, also continue to grow and develop, which brings us to the "plus factor."

IDEA

USE INCLUSIVE PRONOUNS: Using such pronouns as "we," "us," and "our" is much more likely to create a positive classroom environment than using "you," "mine," and "yours." For example, saying "We need to finish the work on time" is preferable to "You students must complete your work." Using the collective term promotes community and shared responsibility.

THE PLUS FACTOR

The artist, like the God of creation,
remains within or behind or above
his handiwork, invisible, refined out of existence,
indifferent, paring his fingernails. (56, p. 215)

When an audience watches the accomplished musician, the headline comedian, the world class athlete, or the master teacher, the intense effort behind the performance becomes invisible. What he or she does seems simple. It is only when members of the audience try to do it themselves that they realize that true art requires endless practice, painstaking effort, personal discipline, and deliberate planning. So it is with invitational teaching.

At its best invitational teaching becomes "invisible." To borrow the words of Chuang-tse, an ancient Chinese philosopher, "It flows like water, reflects like a mirror, and responds like an echo." When the teacher reaches this special plateau of invitational teaching, what he or she does appears effortless. Football teams call it "momentum," comedians refer to it as feeling the "center," world class athletes call it finding the "zone," fighter pilots speak of "rhythm." In invitational teaching we call it the plus factor.

True art is not as readily recognized in teaching as it is in other art forms. When one observes the master teacher, it all looks so easy. The reason is that the master teacher understands that the highest level of teaching is reached when the teacher has mastered the art of being artless. Teaching requires painstaking care, discipline, preparation, and effort; yet it should seem extemporaneous. Somehow when the art is discovered, it reduces its value. Thus, the teacher's long pause, the quick turn, the raised eyebrow, the dramatic gesture, and the surprise conclusion, when carefully honed, appear spontaneous.

An example of the perfection of art is W. C. Fields, the classic comic, who developed a genius for the conscious error. By all accounts, Fields was one of the greatest jugglers that ever lived, and he was gifted in the "retrieved blunder." Fields would drop a hat apparently by accident in the middle of some difficult feat and then catch it by another apparently accidental movement (110). To paraphrase Alexander Pope, true ease in teaching, as in juggling, "comes from art, not chance, as those move easiest who have learn'd to dance."

When Ginger Rogers described dancing with Fred Astaire, she said, "It's a lot of hard work, that I do know." Someone responded: "But it doesn't look it, Ginger." Ginger replied, "That's why it's magic." Invitational teaching, at its best, works like magic. Teachers who master invitational teaching become so fluent that the carefully honed skills and techniques they employ are invisible to the untrained eye. They function with such talented assurance that the tremendous effort involved does not call attention to itself. As Ovid explained in his *Art of Love,* "Ars est celare artem" (Art lies in concealing art). To accomplish this magic mission, teachers employ the *four corner press,* which is the subject of Chapter 4.

IDEA

ASK FOR THE ORDER: There is a skill in asking for what you want without demanding it. Like any skill, it takes practice to ask again (and again) without ordering or commanding. Rather than hinting for what you want in the classroom, ask for it in simple and specific terms. The more explicit an invitation, the more likely it will be received and accepted.

SUMMARY

Chapter 3 has introduced four levels of professional functioning and topped them off with the "plus factor." Level 1, intentionally disinviting, is the domain of those forces that deliberately demean, discourage, and dissuade students. Level 2, unintentionally disinviting, is the land that lacks care or appropriateness. Level 3, unintentionally inviting, is the speciality of the "natural born" teacher. This teacher can describe *what* he or she does, but has difficulty explaining *why*, leading to inconsistency in behavior. Level 4, intentionally inviting, is pictured as a high level of functioning because it is likely to result in positive teaching, learning, and living. Chapter 3 concluded with a description of the "plus factor," described as teaching with such skill and grace that the act of inviting does not call attention to itself.

Chapter 4 will look at the person in the process, the all-important teacher. It will explain the four corner press and will describe how teachers can be more inviting, personally and professionally, with themselves and others.

Chapter 4

THE FOUR CORNER PRESS

Every house worth considering as a work of art must have a grammar of its own. "Grammar," in this sense, means the same thing in any construction—whether it be of words or of stone or wood. It is the shape—relationship between the various elements that enter into the constitution of the thing. The "grammar" of the house is its manifest articulation of all its parts.

—*Frank Lloyd Wright*
The Natural House *(114, p. 181)*

What teachers accomplish in their profession is a function of the persons they are. The highly successful teacher has learned to use one's self in healthy and creative ways. Invitational teaching offers a blueprint for optimal personhood called *the four corner press.*

The term *press* is used in the psychological sense of events and activities that have significance for the individual (79). Each corner represents a vital dimension of personal and professional functioning and offers classroom teachers a realistic way of increasing their IQ (invitational quotient). The four corners are pictured in Figure 3.

Figure 3
The Four Corner Press

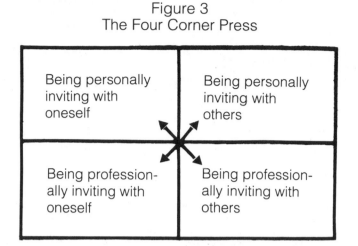

Invitational teaching reminds teachers to orchestrate their lives in each of the four corners to seek harmony and balance in teaching, learning, and living. Like pistons in a finely tuned automobile engine, the four corners work together to give power to the whole movement. While there are times when one of the four corners may demand special attention, the overall goal is synchronization. Each area is vital in invitational teaching because each contributes to a balance between personal and professional functioning.

A healthy balance among the four corners is needed now more than ever. Recent research indicates that it is common for teachers to feel exhausted, estranged, fatigued, powerless, and burned out and to find work meaningless (34, 35, 36, 37, 49). Teachers who practice invitational teaching can, by attending to all four corners, find ways to be enlivened in their teaching, learning, and living.

BEING PERSONALLY INVITING WITH ONESELF

Being personally inviting with oneself precedes the other corners, for personal growth comes before professional growth. It takes an endless variety of forms. It means caring for one's mental health and making appropriate choices in life. By taking up a new hobby, relaxing with a good book, exercising regularly, visiting friends, getting sufficient sleep, growing a garden, or managing time wisely, teachers can rejuvenate their own well-being and develop an ever-expanding understanding of what it means to be fully alive.

IDEA

GET THERE EARLY: There are countless causes of tension and anxiety that are unavoidable. Yet one major cause of teacher tension that can easily be avoided is cutting time too short and running behind. Make a vow to set the alarm a little earlier and arrive at your destination cool, calm, and collected.

Realizing one's own untapped potential is a tremendously important part of invitational teaching. It is difficult for teachers to relate to students if teachers have neglected to relate to themselves. "The single relationship truly central and crucial in a life," states Coudert, "is the relationship to self. It is rewarding to find someone whom you like, but it is essential to like yourself. It is quickening to recognize that someone is a good and decent human being, but it is indispensable to view yourself as acceptable. It is a delight to discover people who are worthy of admiration and respect and love, but it is vital to believe yourself deserving of these things" (33, p.118). When teachers believe that positive relationships are critical to good teaching, they work to establish a positive relationship with themselves. They will seek to stand tall, dress well, eat less, take exercise, become involved, join groups, avoid boredom, laugh more, and find ways to be present in the world. Invitational teaching is the process of using one's self and one's potential to the fullest extent.

It is helpful to keep in mind that the principles of

invitational teaching (trust, respect, optimism, and intentionality) fully apply in being personally inviting with oneself. Perhaps the most important principle is respect for oneself and one's feelings. Feelings are important, and to deny feelings is to deny one's existence. For example, if exercising at night after a hard day in the classroom feels terribly difficult, the teacher might try exercising in the morning. If that does not work, a self-invitation to play a sport, buy an exercise bicycle, or take a walk in the late afternoon or early evening may be appropriate. The secret is to invite oneself in ways that are most likely to be accepted and acted upon. By listening to and respecting one's own feelings and by varying the self-invitations, the probability of success is increased. Inviting oneself personally also requires the seeking of esthetic pleasures. A fresh vase of flowers, a photo or two of loved ones, or a radio with classical music can enrich any classroom.

IDEA

BRIGHTEN YOUR CLASSROOM: Fight drabness and dreariness as much as possible. Even lining up the shades, arranging the chairs in an attractive fashion, and asking for needed repairs (including a fresh coat of paint) can make a happy difference in any classroom.

When the young daughter of one of the authors came home from school her father asked about her homework. When his daughter announced that she did not *have* any homework, the father wanted to know why. In exasperation, the little girl put her hands on her hips and explained: "We don't have any homework because the teacher is out of fluid!" Here are some ways for teachers to avoid running "out of fluid":

- Get tickets to something you have never sampled before (wrestling, opera, ballet, horse show, symphony, football game—the choices are many).

- Dye your hair, get a lift, lose weight, or have your teeth straightened (or whitened).
- Attack your closet and give to charity everything you have not worn in three years.
- Commit yourself to wellness; keeping in shape can become as much a habit as brushing your teeth.
- Try a new breakfast cereal instead of old "facefull."
- Visit a travel agency and load up on travel brochures— dream!
- If you live alone, head for the SPCA and adopt two neutered cats.
- Throw or give away something you don't like.
- Call an old friend you have not talked to in a long time.
- Break a bad habit—just for today.
- Eliminate cigarettes and other substances that are potentially injurious.
- Learn to play a musical instrument badly.
- Throw a party. (You're always invited when you're giving the party.)
- Start a treasury of recognitions, notes, and letters you've received, and read them regularly.

Think of the nicest invitation you could send to another person and send it to yourself.

IDEA

EXPLORE A LIBRARY: For a relaxing and enjoyable experience, spend a few hours browsing in a library. Wander through stacks in areas that you don't usually visit. You will have an exciting world of knowledge at your fingertips— and it costs nothing.

One effective way to invite oneself personally is to monitor what one says to oneself internally and to "clean up" false, demeaning, or negative internal narration. The importance of modifying cognitive processes by monitoring and changing "self-talk" was emphasized by Meichenbaum (74).

As explained by Meichenbaum, the goal is to learn more inviting ways of looking at reality by altering what we say about ourselves to ourselves *internally*—on a semiconscious level. Cognitions affect behavior, and when individuals alter their cognitions, they alter their behavior. For example, by changing such internal dialogue from "always" to "often," from "I must" to "I want," from "problem" to "situation," teachers can inoculate themselves against many environmental stressors.

Beck (11) has identified distortions in thinking that can make one emotionally upset. To improve one's self-talk, one first identifies mental distortions. Among them are *overgeneralization* (assuming that if something happened once, it will certainly happen again), *dichotomous thinking* (perceiving events or people as being one way or another—good or bad), *magnification* (giving more significance to an event than it warrants—"blowing things out of proportion"), *personalization* (constantly comparing oneself with others), *control fantasies* (believing one has no control over life's events or that one must take care of everyone and everything), and *catastrophizing* (concentrating on "what if" something terrible happens and how awful it would be). If the teacher is feeling bad, it may be because he or she is thinking in disinviting ways.

Of course, positive thinking alone is not enough. Research indicates it is the amount of negative thinking that increases emotional distress (11). A decrease in negative thinking is associated with a reduction in emotional distress. An *increase* in positive thinking without a *decrease* in negative thinking has no effect on emotional distress. It is important to identify negative thinking and then work to change these counterproductive thought processes.

56

BEING PERSONALLY INVITING WITH OTHERS

Invitational teaching requires that the feelings, wishes, and aspirations of others be taken into account. Without this requirement, invitational teaching could not exist. In practical terms, this means that the teacher's own well-being is dependent on how concerned the teacher is with the well-being of others. Research on the importance of social networks for professionals has identified a three-part social system that helps buffer stress: support of family and friends, support of co-workers, and support of supervisors (57, 63). Most often, the way to gain support is to give it.

Specific ways to be inviting with others are simple, but sometimes overlooked. Getting to know colleagues on a social basis (the social committee is probably the most important committee in any school), sending friendly notes, remembering birthdays, organizing and enjoying a faculty party, and celebrating the successes of colleagues are all examples of invitational teaching in action. Here are additional ways:

- Remember and use names at every opportunity. (Remembering names shows you care.)
- Keep a card file of people with whom you come in contact, containing special information such as names of spouses and children.

- Promote politeness by always using "Please" and "Thank you" with both spoken and printed communication (such as classroom signs).
- Mark birthdays and other special events on a private calendar in readiness for the special day.
- Share ideas with a friend whose judgment you trust.

In a recent study of inviting teacher behaviors, Amos (5) identified the following activities, clustered into dimensions of personally inviting teacher behaviors:

1. *Commitment*
   a. Disclosing
      - Shares out-of-class experiences
      - Takes time to talk with students about their out-of-class activities
      - Exhibits a sense of humor
   b. Supporting
      - Expresses appreciation for students' presence in class
      - Shows sensitivity to the needs of students
      - Works to encourage students' self-confidence
      - Shows sensitivity to the feelings of students
      - Is willing to help students having special problems

2. *Consideration*
   a. Attending
      - Is polite to students
      - Is easy to talk with
      - Looks students in the eye when talking with them
      - Pauses for several seconds after asking a question
   b. Affirming
      - Shows respect for students
      - Involves students in decision-making processes
      - Promotes a trusting class atmosphere
      - Treats students as though they are responsible
   c. Cheering

- Expresses pleasure with the class
- Acts friendly toward students
- Appears to enjoy life

Amos concluded from her research that there is a high correlation between personally inviting teacher behaviors and student satisfaction with the teacher, the course, and the course content.

IDEA

SHARE WITH FRIENDS: Keep your friends in mind when you receive materials in the mail or read about books or activities relating to their interests. For example, if a friend collects cat figurines, pass on any information about interesting cats. Share magazines, news clips, and brochures that may interest your friends. To care is to act caringly, and almost anything can be used to let your friends know you care.

A special word needs to be offered here regarding friendships, which may be the teacher's primary life-support system. It is through friendships that teachers celebrate their relationships with colleagues, friends, and students. McGinnis (68) offers five ways to deepen friendships:

1. Assign priority to your friendships.
2. Allow others to know you as a person.
3. Talk openly about your affection.
4. Practice the gestures of affection (such as gift giving and rituals).
5. Create space in your relationships so that your friend has room to expand and develop.

These suggestions are only a sample of the countless ways to cultivate friendships. And like gardens, friendships require cultivation to thrive. A friendship without attention is like a plant without water.

BEING PROFESSIONALLY INVITING WITH ONESELF

Being professionally inviting with oneself can take a variety of forms. Trying a new teaching method, seeking certification, learning new computer techniques, returning to graduate school, enrolling in a workshop, attending conferences, reading journals, and writing for publication are just tips of the iceberg.

Invitational teaching encourages teachers not to "rust" on their laurels. Keeping alive professionally is particularly important for teachers because of the rapidly expanding knowledge base regarding teaching and learning. Perhaps never before in North American education have knowledge, techniques, and methods been so bountiful. Recent advances in computer-assisted instruction are breathtaking. The teacher's canoe must be paddled harder than ever just to stay abreast of the knowledge explosion.

IDEA

MAKE DECISIONS EXPEDITIOUSLY: The longer a decision is put off, the more difficult it is to make. It also lessens the amount of time available to correct wrong decisions. Even if you make a wrong decision, it can be a valuable learning experience that leads to adjustment and correction.

Following are practical ways to invite oneself professionally:

- *Be on time.* Punctuality is a sign of intentionality. It

indicates professional caring for yourself and those who depend on your professional involvement.

- *Visit another world.* Explore other vocational settings: businesses, industry, a hospital, or other work settings different from your own. You may collect some good ideas to use in your own work.
- *Begin a museum.* Create a file of letters, awards, or treasures that you have received over time. When you begin to have doubts about yourself, take a tour of your personal museum. It will lift your spirits and renew your faith in your own value, ability, and autonomy.
- *Cool down first.* The professionally inviting teacher avoids responding while angry or upset. It is important to let tempers cool down before answering. Comments exchanged in the heat of battle are often difficult to take back.
- *Manage your time.* Develop a system (a checklist of "things to do" or a schedule of important events to attend) and manage your time accordingly. Budgeting your time helps you expend your energy evenly so that no one area or task consumes all your attention.
- *Visit an exemplary classroom.* Spend some time with a colleague whose work you have heard about at a conference or from some other source.
- *Write it down.* Take time to publicize what you do in your classroom. Write an article for your organization's newsletter, or call the local newspaper and arrange an interview. Put your ideas about teaching on paper so that others may benefit.

These ideas are only samples of what can be done to invite oneself professionally.

One additional thought on being professionally inviting with oneself was contributed by John Novak of Brock University (St. Catherine's, Ontario) in a personal communication. The process of inviting involves not only encounters with students in caring ways. It also involves a teacher's personal relationship with the content and essence of what he or she teaches. A teacher who perceives meaning, clarity, and significance in subject matter is in a far better position to invite students to do likewise. In invitational teaching, having a special love for scholarship is essential.

IDEA

TEACH LESS, BETTER: Concentrate on what is truly important in course content, and teach it well. Some beginning teachers overwhelm students by giving too much, too fast. The formula is "Teach half as much twice as well." Make sure the things you teach stay taught by frequent reviews of important content.

BEING PROFESSIONALLY INVITING WITH OTHERS

The final corner of the four corner press, and the most important to many administrators and parents, is being professionally inviting with others. As Little (67) reported, successful schools are staffed by teachers who are professionally inviting with others. These teachers pursue a broader range of professional interactions and do so with greater frequency.

Among the countless ways that teachers can be professionally inviting with others is to have high aspirations for academic achievement. It also requires that teachers fight sexism and racism in any form, work cooperatively, participate in collegiality, provide professional feedback, and maintain an optimistic "can do" stance in the classroom.

It should be stressed again that invitational teaching does result in student achievement. The evidence is clear and mounting (5, 8, 9) that inviting teachers are successful in promoting student learning. There is no contradiction between inviting teachers and successful ones. When teachers concentrate on self-confidence and self-respect, then students achieve.

In a study of the role of self-concept in academic achievement, Midkiff, Burke, Hunt, and Ellison (75) reported that students' postperformance self-concepts were influenced primarily by their initial self-concepts and, to a lesser extent, by their academic achievement and performance on an academic task. Learning is most likely to result when students feel confident that they can learn and when they look optimistically on their chances for academic success.

IDEA

NO-CUT CONTRACT: Make a "no-cut contract" with students. Everyone agrees that in this classroom

"I will not put you down."
"I will not put myself down."
"You will not put me down."
"You will not put yourself down."

If a student or teacher breaks the contract, he or she is gently reminded of the agreement.

In a series of investigations in a wide range of elementary and secondary classrooms throughout the United States, Aspy, Aspy, and Roebuck (8, 9) explored the relationships among a facilitative climate and both self-concept and academic achievement. They found that classrooms that facilitated self-concept development also enhanced student achievement. These studies included analysis of 200,000 hours of classroom instruction. Samples were taken from classes at all academic levels in forty-two states and seven foreign countries. The clear-cut conclusion from these investigations was that the conditions that enhance self-concept are the very ones that promote academic achievement. Specifically, teachers who respond empathically to their students, who treat them as able, valuable, and responsible; and who present lessons in "do-able" steps promote both emotional and cognitive growth. Conversely, teachers who do not do these things retard student growth in both self-concept and school achievement.

Amos (5) also investigated professionally inviting teacher behaviors and identified the following, clustered into two major dimensions—*coordination* and *proficiency*.

1. *Coordination*
   a. Clarifying
      - Facilitates class discussion without difficulty
      - Summarizes major points of each lesson at the end of class
      - Provides an overview of each lesson
      - Presents a smooth transition from one topic to another
   b. Informing
      - Chooses appropriate readings for the course
      - Uses a variety of methods to help students learn
      - Answers questions clearly
      - Uses tests to evaluate course objectives
      - Is willing to express a lack of knowledge on a subject
      - Evaluates students' work fairly

2. *Proficiency*
   a. Managing
      - Explains grading procedures adequately
      - Demonstrates an up-to-date knowledge of course content
      - Presents understandable class objectives
      - Speaks clearly
      - Presents course content in an organized manner
   b. Relying
      - Comes to class on time

- Is prepared for class
- Is expedient in evaluating students' work
- Ends each class period on time
- Uses class time efficiently

c. Expectation
- Expects high academic performance from students

These professionally inviting qualities seem to be exemplified by a teacher who stated, "I always make an effort to dress for school as if I am going somewhere important."

SUMMARY

Teachers who work to balance and orchestrate the four corners of invitational teaching to create a seamless whole are well on their way to mastering the plus factor of teaching, learning, and living. The inviting teacher is one who artfully blends the four areas in order to sustain energy and enthusiasm.

IDEA

SEND LESSONS C.O.D.: It helps to organize classes around

Content—appropriate, meaningful, solid
Organization—logical, simple, visible
Delivery—interesting, clear, energetic

Students are able to learn material when teachers are able to deliver the course material C.O.D!

Chapter 5

THE FIVE POWERFUL *P*s

> *For men and women are not only themselves;*
> *they are also the region in which they were*
> *born, the city apartment or the farm in which*
> *they learned to walk, the games they played as*
> *children, the old wives' tale they overheard,*
> *the food they ate, the schools they attended, the*
> *sports they followed, the poems they read, and*
> *the God they believed in.*
>
> —*W. Somerset Maugham*
> The Razor's Edge *(71, p.2)*

Invitational teaching is unlike any other viewpoint reported in the professional literature in that it addresses the global nature of the educative process. It provides an overarching framework for a variety of educational programs, policies, and processes that fit with its basic elements presented in Chapter 1.

In invitational teaching there are five powerful *P*s: *people, places, policies, programs,* and *processes,* which are highly significant for their separate and combined influence on what happens in classrooms. Hobbs (47) explained that human problems and promises are not simply with individuals, but also within *ecosystems,* of which the teacher is one part. Rosow and Zager (105) used a similar explanation to indicate that upgrading the performance of a school demands *systemic* changes. That is, not only people, but also the organization as a whole has to change. This includes people, places, policies, programs, and processes that exist in every classroom.

PEOPLE

The classroom teacher is by far the most important factor in establishing the culture of the classroom. Moskowits and Hayman (78) conducted two separate investigations of teachers in urban junior high schools. The first investigation provided detailed observations of teachers during the first months of the school year. The second study included more teachers and a longer time period (the entire year). The results of both studies were much the same. Successful teachers worked from the very beginning to build an inviting classroom environment. They established and maintained "warm, understanding, supportive climates in which students felt comfortable and were able to work productively" (78, p. 288).

IDEA

CHECK THE CLASS PULSE: Look around the classroom and observe student activity and energy levels. What is in the air? Is something special needed to get students focused on class material? Monitor the mood and energy level of students to determine the best thing to do at this moment to get students involved in learning.

In a review of a wide range of studies on classroom organization, Brophy (15) provided detailed descriptions of how successful teachers established supportive environments. Effective teachers consistently demonstrated three clusters of behaviors: "conveying purposefulness," "teaching appropriate behaviors," and "diagnosing students' focus of attention." They conveyed purposefulness by expressing concern for instruction and by circulating throughout the classroom to monitor student progress and provide feedback. They exhibited appropriate behaviors by communicating expectations clearly and by stressing appropriate behavior. They diagnosed the students' focus of attention by being sensitive to the students' confusion and inattention.

The picture that emerges from descriptions of teachers who practice invitational teaching is one of caring, sensitive, active people who understand their students and who find numerous ways to invite students to realize their potential.

Here are some practical ways to highlight the importance of people in invitational teaching:

- Organize a wellness program, with health checks, group walking, and an aerobics class after school.
- Plan a faculty talent show and take part.
- Arrange a room parent seminar with a bring-a-dish supper.
- Have a special dress day with a designated theme (blue dress day for "test-busting").
- Print up teacher business cards that read "Professional Teacher."
- Organize a faculty breakfast bimonthly.
- Maintain a bulletin board that features a different student each week.
- Organize a one-day faculty retreat to build morale.

PLACES

The people in the classroom are of paramount importance, but places also play an important role. Visitors to schools and classrooms have long noted that certain classrooms feel "sunny" and inviting. Others, even those that might be modern and well furnished, feel "gloomy" and disinviting. Although research evidence is lacking to show that the physical environment of the classroom relates directly to academic achievement, Rutter, Maughan, Mortimore, and Ouston (106) did report that a school's physical environment relates to pupil behavior. They proposed that students, like teachers, recognize that an inviting physical environment is one way in which teachers show concern for students. An example of an inviting place is a junior high school with a welcome sign—in ten languages. Here are some practical indicators of inviting and disinviting classrooms:

Inviting	Disinviting
Fresh paint	Full trash cans
Pleasant smell	Harsh lighting
Attractive bulletin boards	Excessive noise
Lots of books	Bare walls
Sanitary environment	Broken desks and chairs
Flowers on the desk	Out-of-date bulletin boards
Sunny room	A full pencil sharpener
Matching colors	Straight rows
Positively worded signs	Peeling paint and plaster
Clean windows	Stuffy room
Living green plants	Broken windows
Comfortable temperature	Disorganized materials
Attractive pictures	Dusty, cobwebby shelves
Conveniently located trash cans	Litter on floor
Well-arranged furniture	Cluttered teacher's desk
Current student displays	Torn, uneven shades
Window bird feeder	Graffiti
Good ventilation	Institutional paint

Most of the above can be positively influenced by teachers who practice invitational teaching.

In case studies of exemplary schools, Lipsitz (66) concluded that the physical environment of the school contributes to good student behavior by encouraging students to feel ownership in the classroom and by organizing the physical space to minimize disruptions. In each school Lipsitz studied, the students interviewed described things they did that made them feel the school was "theirs." They named things like decorating the classroom, helping build things for the classroom, and helping keep things clean and unmarked. When Johnston (52), in an investigation of school climate, interviewed students, he asked, "How do you know the school cares about you and your learning?" Students most often mentioned the cleanliness of the school.

IDEA

PAINT SOME MURALS: Any blank wall in a classroom can be brightened with larger-than-life murals. Murals can be done on large sheets of white paper taped to the wall or on chalkboards, using the opaque projector and a group of students with markers. The project teaches cooperation, and the beautiful results give students pride in their classroom environment.

POLICIES

The third powerful *P* deals with the policies created and maintained in classrooms. Policies are everywhere, including those established by school boards, superintendents, principals, and others, but classroom policies have the greatest impact. "Rules" regarding conduct constitute a major dimension of classroom policies.

In their review of research on classroom management, Brophy and Putnam (17) contended that "effective management requires a workable set of classroom rules and procedures" (p. 196). Brophy and Putnam also contended that rules should be minimized and phrased in terms of general aspects of behavior, rather than long lists of "do's" and "don'ts." They maintained that rules should be flexible to allow changes as situations demand.

In an analysis of exemplary schools, Johnston (52) reported that the schools he visited had few rules, but those rules that did exist were clear and reasonable. He also noted that positive rules are much more useful: for example, "Respect people, respect property" is much more useful than "No hitting" or "No slamming of locker doors." In the schools that Johnston studied, brief lists of positive rules provided a basis for common agreement by students and teachers.

Written policies themselves do not appear to be as critical as the common classroom expectations of students and teacher. Whether the policies are written or not, everyone in the classroom should be able to expect the same standard of respect. Rules and policies are for students *and* teachers. Students are more likely to respect the rules if teachers also abide by them. Inviting teachers wait their turn. When Lipsitz (66) asked middle-level students how they knew what the policies were, even though they were not written down, students replied that they learned them from experiences, from the examples the teacher set, and from the teacher's praise of good behavior.

Sometimes students and teachers are influenced by the rules, regulations, orders, plans, and policies imposed from above, and often created with little or no regard for teacher or student need, developmental level, or individual situation. These policies, while often well intended, can place unfair and unreasonable restrictions on teachers and students alike. An example of a counterproductive policy might be mandatory suspension for certain offenses, regardless of the circumstances. Using suspension as a school policy has the unhappy result that it removes students from the very places where they might learn to behave. It also places the student behind in schoolwork, which leads to academic failure.

A 1988 statewide study of school dropout factors in the secondary schools of North Carolina demonstrated that attempts to counter high dropout rates through stricter policies have not proved to be successful (98). Classroom policies should be created and maintained in light of the welfare of the student.

Here are some useful classroom policies:

- Return parent phone calls immediately.
- Keep parents notified (of student achievements, concerns, attendance, etc.).
- Develop a "buddy system" for new students.
- Assign "can do" homework that *all* students are able to complete.
- Teach something tough, that takes considerable time to learn, that students will take pride in knowing.
- Teach to pass, coach to win.

IDEA

KEEP IT SIMPLE, SWEETHEART (KISS): Teachers who propose a large number of classroom rule are ensuring that rules will be broken. The fewer rules there are, the fewer chances there are to break them. A few good rules can be agreed on by students and teacher and are likely to be in the best interests of everyone.

PROGRAMS

Programs in classrooms consist of all those curricular and extracurricular activities designed to meet the needs of students. But, like policies, some programs can be counterproductive. Programs that label students as being "different" can negatively influence the beneficial purposes for which these programs were originally intended.

Recent programs that have received wide recognition and approval include those that foster cooperative learning. Cooperative learning is a team approach to the educative process. Teachers first make sure students have learned basic social and verbal skills so that they learn from discussion and group processing (51).

Cooperative student groups may vary in size, although

four-member teams are often used. Group members are chosen so that students at different levels of achievement are placed together. Often, the highest-achieving student, the lowest-achieving student, and two students achieving at an "average" level are placed together. Another group might include the student who is the second highest achiever in class, the next to the lowest achiever in class, and two who achieve at a middle level. This group arrangement provides extra help for students who need it and an opportunity for higher-achieving students to learn by teaching.

Cooperative learning emphasizes the importance of group and individual accountability. Specific measures are taken to ensure that students within the group meet individual learning goals. Also, students are given a "group grade," indicating their efforts to work together. In addition to external measures of learning content, group process is also evaluated, with the teacher suggesting ideas for improvement when necessary.

This cooperative learning approach can be used to review for tests, to apply concepts and theories, and to complete special projects or practice specific skills. Because cooperative groups are not discussion groups, their size will vary with the task to be completed. Cooperative learning works with students of all ages and abilities.

From an invitational teaching viewpoint, any program introduced in any classroom is to be tested against the basic assumptions of invitational education: Do these programs show trust, respect, optimism, and intentionality? Do they communicate to students that they are able, valuable, and responsible? Cooperative learning scores extremely well when measured against these standards.

Following are some additional ways to develop inviting classroom programs:

- Organizing a parent/grandparent tutoring program
- Creating academic and special interest clubs (selected

by students)

- Inviting successful graduates of the school to visit the class and talk with students
- Encouraging special assembly programs to recognize various cultures
- Starting a science or math Olympiad
- Beginning a higher-order thinking skills program
- Introducing a ROPES course to encourage classroom teamwork
- Developing a yearlong class project
- Scheduling presentations by local experts
- Creating a "Gold Credit Card" for student academic improvement or honor roll students

IDEA

CELEBRATE DIVERSITY: Students and teachers may represent different regions, life styles, and ethnic origins. This diversity presents a rich opportunity for students and teachers to learn the customs, traditions, and heritage of others. Students learn to understand other students better and enjoy sharing experiences and perceptions. Diversity can be celebrated by special meals, festivals, assemblies, and storytelling hours.

PROCESSES

Processes, the final powerful *P,* is an inseparable part of the people, places, policies, and programs of the classroom. Yet process is so critical in and of itself that it deserves special mention. Process represents not so much content as *context.* It represents the melody of the classroom. As the old bromide attests, it is not *what* is done, but *how* it is done, that makes the difference.

A critical difference between effective and ineffective

teachers is the degree to which the teacher attends to the social side of learning—the process of working together toward common goals based on mutually established purposes. Attending to the social side of learning is recognizing that *how* teachers teach and *how* they act are as important as who they are or what they teach. Invitational teaching is the process of using one's self and one's knowledge in creative and healthy ways.

Some inviting processes include the following:

- Giving students clear responsibilities (collecting materials, arranging the classroom, tidying up, etc.)
- Holding mock elections, trials, debates, and role plays to encourage democratic values
- Having students teach students in a helping relationship
- Seeking consensus when making decisions
- Providing peer counseling
- Having students evaluate teachers and teachers evaluate teachers
- Graduating the difficulty of course content

IDEA

LAUGH A LITTLE: Classrooms can be hilarious places. Teachers and students often say funny things they don't intend to say or notice humor in something being studied. Laughter warms a classroom. Teachers and students who "goof something up" in the classroom can share their humanness by laughing at the situation.

SUMMARY

Judging by the five Powerful *P*s, invitational teaching is an extremely complex matrix of human experiences. Each of the five *P*s is essential for the other four because they interlock. They work as one unit to create a dynamic force for the development of human potential. Policies mean little if they are punitive and based on maintaining power instead of encouraging the development of responsible behavior. Programs fall short of their intended goals if they are limited to the interests of only a few teachers or students. Places that are beautiful can promote a sense of aesthetics only if the people who live there choose to work together as a team and appreciate each other's talents and diversity.

The classroom and everything in it, including the people, places, policies, programs, and processes, are like one big bowl of jello: Touch it anywhere and the whole thing jiggles. The jello analogy helps the teacher to remember that *everything*—temperature, time of day, color of walls, the teacher's clothing—adds to or subtracts from invitational teaching. No effort to make the classroom more inviting is wasted. The teacher who practices invitational teaching works on each of the five *P*s persistently.

Chapter 6

CONFLICT RESOLUTION: THE RULE OF THE FIVE *C*s

> *When Yen Ho was about to take up his duties as tutor to the heir of Ling, Duke of Wei, he went to Ch'u Po Yu for advice. "I have to deal with a man of depraved and murderous disposition. . . . How is one to deal with a man of this sort?"*
>
> *"I am glad," said Ch'u Po Yu, "that you asked this question. . . . The first thing you must do is not to improve him, but to improve yourself."*
>
> —*Ancient Taoist story (13)*

Teachers who practice invitational teaching face the need to resolve vexing conflicts, handle difficult situations, and maintain discipline the same as anyone else in schools or society. The purpose of invitational teaching is to resolve these situations with respect for the dignity and worth of everyone involved. This final chapter presents an invitational teaching approach to conflict resolution by describing what teachers can do to resolve conflicts at the lowest possible level, with the least amount of energy, with the minimal possible costs, and in the most humane and respectful manner. To do this, the rule of the five *C*s is employed. The rule is to play, whenever possible, the lowest *C* level first, and move upward through higher *C*s only as necessary.

The five *C*s are *concern, confer, consult, confront,* and *combat.* In any situation where there may be differences of opinion, where rules may be broken, or where discipline may be needed, the first thought should be "How can I resolve this

79

situation at the lowest possible *C* level?" Any teacher can escalate a situation into a conflict. It takes knowledge, effort, and intentionality to resolve a situation with the lowest C, beginning with *concern.*

> ### IDEA
>
> *PRACTICE HALT:* Whenever possible, try not to make decisions when you are
> *H*ungry
> *A*ngry
> *L*onely
> *T*ired
>
> Under HALT conditions, it is easy to misread or overreact to classroom events. Waiting one day, or taking time to cool off, may make a positive difference.

CONCERN

In any situation where there is the potential for conflict, the teacher who practices invitational teaching asks him- or herself

- Is this situation really a concern? Can it safely and wisely be overlooked?
- Will this situation solve itself without intervention?
- Does this situation involve a matter of fairness, principles, or values?
- Is this situation a concern because of *personal* biases, prejudices, or hang-ups?
- Is this the proper time to be concerned with this situation?
- Is there anything that can possibly be done about this situation?
- Are there sufficient resources, support, and informa-

tion available to successfully address the situation?

- Will ignoring it bring stress or create greater concern?

Often situations can be successfully addressed at this lowest level by reconceptualizing the concern. A silly wisecrack offered by a student in response to a question might be an occasion more for mutual laughter than for confrontation. Of course, there are times when a situation is of sufficient concern to require action. These are times when the teacher proceeds to the second *C: confer.*

IDEA

RECONCEPTUALIZE THE SITUATION: Often concerns appear unsolvable because the situation is viewed from only one vantage point. Changing conceptions can change situations. For example, a student with a high energy level can be a problem, but he or she can also be a valuable source of assistance to the teacher.

CONFER

To confer means to initiate an informal conversation with the student or other person *in private*. Begin by signaling the desire for a positive interaction (a smile, using the person's name, eye contact, a handshake, some small expression of pleasure). Then state, in a nonthreatening and respectful way, *what* the concern is, *why* it is a concern, and *what* is proposed to resolve the concern. For example, "Mary, running in the hall is dangerous. You might injure someone running. Please walk rather than run in the hallway." Or "John, coming late to class is distracting. It interrupts the class lesson. I will appreciate your promptness in coming to class." After the statement is made, follow it up immediately by asking: "Will you do this for me?" It is important to ask for what is wanted. No one can read minds.

At the conferring level, it is important to consider these questions:

- Do both parties clearly understand what the concern is?
- Do both parties know *why* the situation is a concern?
- Is it clear *what* is wanted?
- Does the concern relate to mutually established classroom goals?
- Is there room for compromise or joint reconceptualization of the situation?
- Is there time to allow the parties to reflect on the concern before further actions are taken?
- Is the concern important enough to move to a higher *C*, if necessary?

In most situations, a one-on-one, nonthreatening informal conference will successfully eliminate the concern. When conferring does not work, the third *C—consult—*is appropriate.

IDEA

BE A BULLDOG: It is critical to let students know that the teacher will not give up on them. For example, when a student does not turn in an assignment, the persistent teacher says, "This assignment is important. When will you get it in?" It is not a matter of *if.* The student has clear responsibilities. The assignment may be late, but it *will* come in.

CONSULT

Consultation requires a formal discussion with the parties involved. Because this consultation usually involves talking about what has already been discussed, it requires firmness and directness. For example, "John, last week you said that you would come to class on time, yet this morning you were late. This is creating problems for you and for me." In consultation, the focus is on abiding by commitments that were made in the previous conference: "You told me that you would come to class on time and I expect you to keep your word."

Questions that should be considered at the consultation stage include

- Is it clear to all parties what is expected? Are all cards on the table?
- Are there ways to assist the parties in abiding by previous decisions?
- Have the consequences of not resolving the situation been considered?

While a direct and deliberate discussion may not resolve the situation, it gives clear notice of its significance. If the situation persists, then it is time for the fourth *C: confront.*

IDEA

IDENTIFY THE DIFFERENCE: There is a vast difference between "rejection" and "nonacceptance." That a student has not accepted the teacher's request does not mean that the student has rejected it. Sometimes a little patience and time can make all the difference. The world was not created in a day, and neither are people.

CONFRONT

Confronting is a no-nonsense attempt to work out a difficult situation that is of major concern. At this fourth stage, it is important *again* to spell out in careful detail the continuing situation. Describe what the situation is and why it is of major

83

concern. Point out that this situation has been addressed previously and repeatedly, and that progress has been insufficient. Now is the time to speak of unavoidable penalties. For example: "John, if you are late for class again, I will contact your parents." By spelling out logical consequences, everyone understands the rules of the game. Questions that might be asked at this fourth stage include

- Have sincere efforts been made to resolve the situation at each of the lower levels?
- Is there documented evidence to show earlier efforts to resolve the situation at lower levels?
- Is there sufficient authority and power to follow through with stated penalties?
- Will confronting help to solve the situation?

When consequences involving penalties occur, and when the rule of the five *C*s has been followed, all parties are likely to know that the consequences were fair and impartial—which leads to the final *C: combat.*

COMBAT

As used here, the word *combat* is defined as struggling against in order to reduce or eliminate the concern, as to combat inflation, to combat racism, and to combat misbehavior. It is used as a verb rather than a noun, as in the sense of active fighting or warfare. The goal is to combat the situation, not the person.

The use of the word *combat* stresses the seriousness of the situation. It also means that because the situation has not been resolved at lower levels, it is now time to move into the highest *C*.

For obvious reasons, combat is to be avoided wherever possible. At the combat level, there are likely to be winners and losers. In significant contests, it is often unpredictable who will win and who will lose. Moreover, combat requires a great deal of energy that might be better used in more productive endeavors. Yet when all else fails, and the situation is of sufficient concern, then it is time to enter the arena. In preparing for combat, it is helpful to consider the following:

- Is there clear documentation that avenues other than combat were sought?
- Even at this late date, is there a way to avoid combat?
- Are sufficient support and resources available to win the contest?
- How can the winner demonstrate compassion for the loser?

At the successful conclusion of the contest, the educator should end things up with as much fairness and sympathy as possible.

Respect is a basic ingredient of invitational teaching. Even when the most serious penalties must be leveled against a student, the feeling should be of sadness rather than vengeful joy. At the end of a great naval battle, when British sailors were crowded on the deck of their ship, cheering the final death struggle of the great German battleship, Bismarck, a British naval officer reminded his men: "Don't cheer, men. Those poor souls are dying." It is sad when teacher and students reach the combat stage, and any penalties are to be administered with as much respect and compassion as possible.

By solving concerns at the lowest possible level, teachers who employ invitational teaching save energy, reduce conflict, and avoid acrimony. Again, any teacher can go from persuasion to coercion; all it takes is raw power. But no one is without power. The teacher who practices invitational teaching understands that everyone has power, no matter how small they are or what position they hold. Because power is shared, the inviting teacher always uses the lowest possible *C* to resolve concerns.

SUMMARY

This monograph has introduced invitational teaching and explored the marvelous process of inviting school success for everyone. It identified the vital elements of invitational teaching: trust, respect, optimism, and intentionality. It explained the four levels of functioning and introduced the plus factor. It continued with the four corner press, which stresses the importance of harmony and balance in personal and professional living. It then presented the five powerful *P*s: people, places, policies, programs, and processes. The monograph concluded with some practical strategies for conflict resolution built around the five *C*s.

BIBLIOGRAPHY

1. Allport, G. W. 1937. *Personality: A psychological interpretation.* New York: Holt, Rinehart & Winston.

2. Allport, G. W. 1943. The ego in contemporary psychology. *Psychological Review* 50: 451–78.

3. Allport, G. W. 1955. *Becoming.* New Haven, Conn.: Yale University Press.

4. Allport, G. W. 1961. *Pattern and growth in personality.* New York: Holt, Rinehart & Winston.

5. Amos, L. 1985. Professionally and personally inviting teacher practices as related to affective course outcomes reported by dental hygiene students. Ph.D. diss., School of Education, University of North Carolina at Greensboro.

6. Arnold, V. and T. Roach. 1989. Teaching: A nonverbal communication event. *Business Education Forum* 44: 18–20.

7. Aspy, D. N. 1972. *Toward a technology for humanizing education.* Champaign, Ill.: Research Press.

8. Aspy, D., C. Aspy, and F. Roebuck. 1985. *Third century in American education.* Amherst, Mass.: Human Resources Development Press.

9. Aspy, D., and F. Roebuck. 1977. *Kids don't learn from people they don't like.* Amherst, Mass.: Human Resources Development Press.

10. Avila, D., and W. W. Purkey. 1966. Intrinsic and extrinsic motivation: A regrettable distinction. *Psychology in the schools* 3: 206–208.

11. Beck, A. 1976. *Cognitive therapy and the emotional disorders.* New York: International Universities Press.

12. Beck, A., and G. Emery. 1985. *Anxiety disorders and phobias: A cognitive perspective.* New York: Basic Books.

13. Bennis, W., and B. Nanus. 1985. *Leaders: The strategies for taking charge.* New York: Harper & Row.

14. Bergman, K., and T. Gaitskill. 1990. Faculty and student perceptions of effective clinical teachers. *Journal of Professional Nursing.* 6 (1): 33–44.

15. Brophy, J. E. 1983. Classroom organization and management. *Elementary School Journal* 83: 265–85.

16. Brophy, J. 1987. Synthesis of research on strategies for motivating students to learn. *Educational Leadership* 45: 40–48.

17. Brophy, J. E., and J. G. Putnam. 1979. Classroom management in the elementary grades. In *Classroom management,* ed. D. Duke, 182–216. Chicago: University of Chicago Press.

18. Byrne, B. M. and R. J. Shavelson. 1987. Adolescent self-concept: Testing the assumption of equivalent structure across gender. *American Educational Research Journal* 24, 365–86.

19. Carnegie Foundation for the Advancement of Teaching. 1991. *The condition of teaching: A state-by-state analysis.* A Carnegie Foundation Technical Report. Washington, D.C.: The Carnegie Foundation.

20. Chamberlin, J. G. 1981. *The educating act: A phenomenological view.* Washington, D.C.: University Press of America.

21. Clawson, K. and J. Paterno. 1987. Inferred self-concept as learner as it relates to reading achievement and gender: Kindergarten and First Grade Student. Paper presented at the annual meeting of the Mid-South Educational Research Association, Mobile, Alabama.

22. Combs, A. W. 1949. A phenomenal approach to adjustment theory. *Journal of Abnormal and Social Psychology* 44: 29–35.

23. Combs, A. W., ed. 1962. *Perceiving, behaving, becoming.* Washington, D.C.: Association for Supervision and Curriculum Development.

24. Combs, A. W. 1965. *The professional education of teachers: A perceptual view of teacher preparation.* Boston: Allyn & Bacon.

25. Combs, A. W. 1974. Why the humanist movement needs a perceptual psychology. *Journal of the Association for the Study of Perception* 9: 1–13.

26. Combs, A. W. 1982. *A personal approach to teaching: Beliefs that make a difference.* Boston: Allyn & Bacon.

27. Combs, A. W. and D. Avila. 1984. *The helping relationship.* 3d ed. Boston: Allyn & Bacon.

28. Combs, A. W., D. L. Avila, and W. W. Purkey. 1978. *Helping relationships: Basic concepts for the helping professions.* 2d ed. Boston: Allyn & Bacon.

29. Combs, A. W., A. C. Richards, and F. Richards. 1976. *Perceptual psychology: A humanistic approach to the study of persons.* New York: Harper & Row.

30. Combs, A. W., and D. Snygg. 1959. *Individual behavior: A perceptual approach to behavior.* 2d ed. New York: Harper & Row.

31. Cooley, C. H. 1902 *Human nature and the social order.* New York: Charles Scribner's Sons.

32. Coopersmith, S. 1967. *The antecedents of self-esteem.* San Francisco: Freeman.

33. Coudert, J. 1965. *Advice from a failure.* New York: Dell.

34. Dworkin, A. G. 1985. *When teachers give up: Teacher burnout, teacher turnover, and their impact on children.* Austin: Hogg Foundation for Mental Health and Texas Press.

35. Dworkin, A. G. 1987. *Teacher burnout in the public schools: Structural causes and consequences for children.* New York: State University of New York.

36. Dworkin, A. G., C. Allen Haney, R. Dworkin, and R. Telschow. 1990. Stress and illness behavior among urban public school teachers. *Educational Administration Quarterly* 26: 60–72.

37. Dworkin, A. G., C. A. Haney, and R. Telschow. 1988. Fear, victimization, and stress among urban public school teachers. *Journal of Organizational Behavior* 9: 159-71.

38. Festinger, L. 1962. *A theory of cognitive dissonance.* New York: Harper & Row.

39. Fitts, W. 1965. *Tennessee self concept scale.* Nashville: Counselor Recordings and Tests.

40. Galbo, J. 1989. The teacher as significant adult: A review of the literature. *Adolescence* 24: 549–56.

41. Goffin, Stacie. 1989. How well do we respect the children in our care? *Childhood Education* 66: 68–74.

42. Good, T., and J. Brophy. 1987. *Looking in classrooms.* 4th ed. New York: Harper & Row.

43. Harper, K. L. 1989. *An investigation of inferred and professed self-concept-as-learner of gifted and average middle school students.* Ph.D. diss., University of North Carolina at Greensboro.

44. Harper, K., and W. W. Purkey. 1990. *Inferred and professed self-concept-as-learner of gifted and average middle school students across three grade levels.* Greensboro: School of Education, University of North Carolina at Greensboro.

45. Harter, S. 1988. Causes, correlates, and the functional role of global self-worth: A life span perspective. In *Perceptions of competence and incompetence across the life-span*, J. Kolligian and R. Sternberg, ed. New Haven, Conn.: Yale University Press.

46. Helmke, A. 1987. *Mediating processes between children's self-concept of ability and mathematics achievement: A longitudinal study*. Munich: Max-Planck-Institute for Psychological Research.

47. Hobbs, N. 1982. *The troubled and troubling child*. San Francisco: Jossey-Bass.

48. Inglis, S. C. 1976. The development and validation of an instrument to assess teacher invitations and teacher effectiveness as reported by students in a technical and general post-secondary setting. Ph. D. diss. University of Florida, Gainesville.

49. Ivanicki, E. F., and R. L. Schwab. 1987. A cross-validation of the Maslach Burnout Inventory. *Educational and Psychological Measurement* 41: 1167–74.

50. Ivey, A. 1977. Cultural expertise: Toward systematic outcome criteria in counseling and psychological education. *Personnel and Guidance Journal* 55: 296–302.

51. Johnson, D. W., and R. T. Johnson. 1989. *Leading the cooperative school*. Edina, Minn.: Interaction Book Co.

52. Johnston, H. J., with J. Maria Ramos de Perez. 1985. Four climates of effective middle schools. In *Schools in the middle*, 1–8. Washington, D.C.: National Association of Secondary School Principals.

53. Jong, E. 1977. *How to save your own life*. New York: Holt, Rinehart, & Winston.

54. Jourard, S. 1971a. *Self-disclosure: An experimental analysis of the transparent self*. New York: Wiley-Interscience.

55. Jourard, S. 1971b. *The transparent self: Self-disclosure and*

well-being. Rev. ed. Princeton, N.J.: Van Nostrand.

56. Joyce, J. 1916. *A portrait of the artist as a young man.* New York: Viking Press.

57. Kaplan, H. B. 1983. Psychological distress in sociological context: Toward a general theory of psychological distress. In *Psychological stress: Trends in theory and research,* H. B. Kaplan, ed. 195–264. New York: Academic Press.

58. Kelly, G. A. 1955. *The psychology of personal constructs.* New York: W. W. Norton & Co.

59. Kelly, G. A. 1963. *Theory of personality: The psychology of personal contructs.* New York: W. W. Norton & Co.

60. Kohut, H. 1971. *The analysis of self.* New York: International Universities Press.

61. Lambeth, C. R. 1980. Teacher invitations and effectiveness as reported by secondary students in Virginia. Ph.D. diss. University of Virginia, Charlottesville.

62. Landfried, S. 1989. "Enabling" undermines responsibility in students. *Educational Leadership.* 47: 79–83.

63. Larocco, J. M., J. S. House, and J. R. French, Jr. 1980. Social support, occupational stress, and health. *Journal of Health and Social Behavior* 21: 202–18.

64. Lecky, P. 1945. *Self-consistency: A theory of personality.* New York: Island Press.

65. Lewis, J. 1986. *Achieving excellence in our schools: By taking lessons from America's best-run companies.* Westbury, N.Y.: J. L. Wilkerson Pub.

66. Lipsitz, J. 1984. *Successful schools for young adolescents.* New Brunswick, N.J.: Transaction Books.

67. Little, J. W. 1982. Norms of collegiality and experimentation: Workplace conditions of school success. *American Educational Research Journal* 19: 325–340.

68. McGinnis, A. L. 1979. *The friendship factor*. Minneapolis: Augsburg Publishing House.

69. Mahoney, M. J. 1985. Psychotherapy and human change processes. In *Cognition and psychotherapy*, ed. Michael Mahoney and Arthur Freeman, 3–48. New York: Plenum Press.

70. Maslow, A. 1956. *The self: Explorations in personal growth*. New York: Harper & Row.

71. Maugham, W. S. 1944. *The razor's edge*. New York: Doubleday.

72. Mead, G. H. 1934. *Mind, self, and society*. Chicago: University of Chicago Press.

73. Meichenbaum, D. 1974. Cognitive behavior modification. *University programs modular studies*. Morristown, N.J.: General Learning Press.

74. Meichenbaum, D. 1977. *Cognitive behavior modification: An integrative approach*. New York: Plenum Press.

75. Midkiff, R. M., J. P. Burke, J. P. Hunt, and C. C. Ellison. 1986. Role of self-concept of academic attainment in achievement-related behaviors. *Psychological Reports* 58: 151–59.

76. Milne, A. A. 1926. *Winnie—the Pooh* New York: E.P. Dutton.

77. Mizer, J. E. 1964. Cipher in the snow. *NEA Journal* 53: 8–10.

78. Moskowits, G., and M. Hayman. 1976. Success strategies of inner-city teachers: A yearlong study. *Journal of Educational Research* 69: 283–89.

79. Murray, H. 1938. *Explorations in personality*. New York: Oxford University Press.

80. O'Keefe, P. and M. Johnston. 1989. Perspective taking and teacher effectiveness: A connecting thread through three developmental literatures. *Journal of Teacher Education* 40 (3): 20–26.

81. Ouchi, W. G. 1981. *Theory Z: How American business can meet the Japanese challenge.* Reading, Mass.: Addison-Wesley.

82. Patterson, C. H. 1959. *Counseling and psychotherapy: Theory and practice.* New York: Harper & Row.

83. Patterson, C. H. 1961. The self in recent Rogerian theory. *Journal of Individual Psychology* 17: 5–11.

84. Patterson, C. H. 1962. *Counseling and guidance in schools: A first course.* New York: Harper & Row.

85. Patterson, C. H. 1973. *Humanistic Education.* Englewood Cliffs, N.J.: Prentice-Hall.

86. Patterson, C. H. 1985a. New light for counseling theory. *Journal of Counseling and Development* 63: 349–50.

87. Patterson, C. H. 1985b. *The therapeutic relationship: Foundations for an eclectic Psychotherapy.* Monterey: Brooks/Cole.

88. Patterson, C. H. 1986. *Theories of counseling and psychotherapy.* New York: Harper & Row.

89. Peck, S. 1978. *The road less traveled.* New York: Simon & Schuster.

90. Piers, E., and D. Harris. 1969. *The Piers-Harris children's self-concept scale.* Nashville, Tenn.: Counselor Recordings and Tests.

91. Purkey, W. W. 1970. *Self-concept and school achievement.* Englewood Cliffs, N.J.: Prentice-Hall.

92. Purkey, W. W. 1978. *Inviting school success.* Belmont, Calif.: Wadsworth.

93. Purkey, W. W., and J. Novak. 1984. *Inviting school success.* 2d ed. Belmont, Calif.: Wadsworth.

94. Purkey, W. W., and J. Novak. 1988. *Education: By invitation only.* Bloomington, Ind.:Phi Delta Kappa Educational Foundation. Fastback 268.

95. Purkey, W. W., and J. J. Schmidt. 1987. *The inviting relationship.* Englewood Cliffs, N.J.: Prentice-Hall.

96. Purkey, W. W., and J. Schmidt. 1990. *Invitational learning for counseling and development.* Ann Arbor, Mich.: ERIC/CAPS.

97. Purkey, W. W., and D. Strahan. 1986. *Positive discipline: A pocketful of ideas.* Columbus, Ohio: National Middle School Association.

98. Research and Evaluation Associates, Inc. 1988. *Study of school dropout factors in the secondary schools of North Carolina.* Chapel Hill, N. C.: Research and Evaluation Associates.

99. Ripley, D. M. 1985. Invitational teaching behaviors in the associate degree clinical setting. Master's thesis, School of Nursing, University of North Carolina at Greensboro.

100. Rogers, C. R. 1961. *On becoming a person: A therapist's view of psychotherapy.* Boston: Houghton Mifflin.

101. Rogers, C. R. 1967. *Coming into existence.* New York: World Publishing.

102. Rogers, C. R. 1969. *Freedom to learn* Columbus, Ohio: Charles E. Merrill.

103. Rogers, C. R. 1974. In retrospect—forty-six years. *American Psychologist* 29: 115.

104. Rogers, C. R. 1980. *A way of being.* Boston: Houghton Mifflin.

105. Rosow, J. M., and R. Zager. 1989. *Allies in educational reform.* San Francisco: Jossey-Bass.

106. Rutter, M., B. Maughan, P. Mortimore, and J. Ouston. 1979. *Fifteen thousand hours: Secondary schools and their effects on children.* Cambridge: Harvard University Press.

107. Saint-Exupéry, Antoine de. 1943. *The little prince.* New York: Harcourt Brace Jovanovich.

108. Short, P., and R. Short. 1988. Perceived classroom environment of student behavior in secondary schools. *Educational Research Quarterly* 12 (3): 35–39.

109. Smith, C. F. 1987. The effect of selected teaching practices on affective outcomes of graduate nursing students: An extension and replication. Master's thesis, School of Nursing, University of North Carolina at Greensboro.

110. Taylor, R. L. 1949. *W. C. Fields: His follies and fortunes.* Garden City, N.Y.: Doubleday.

111. Turner, R. B. 1983. Teacher invitations and effectiveness as reported by physical education students, grades 9-12. Ph. D. diss., University of North Carolina at Greensboro.

112. Uttal, W. R. 1981. *A taxonomy of visual processes.* Hillsdale, N.J.: Erlbaum.

113. Wigington, H., N. Tollefson, E. Rodriguez. 1989. Students' ratings of instructors revisited: Interactions among class and instructor variables. *Research in Higher Education* 30 (3): 331–44.

114. Wright, F. L. 1954. *The natural house.* New York: Horizon Press.

115. Wylie, R. 1961. *The self-concept: A critical survey of pertinent research literature.* Lincoln: University of Nebraska Press.

116. Wylie, R. 1979. *The self-concept: Vol. 2, Theory and research on selected topics.* Lincoln: University of Nebraska Press.